N. Carolina

the Confederate States of America, | PAY ROLL of the Company, from the 1st day of May 1864, when last
f June 186 4 | paid, to the 30th day of June 1864.

1700
100k

15 18 53

an leo n 6

PERIOD PAID FOR.		PAY PER MONTH.	AMOUNT OF PAY.		COMMUTATION FOR SIX MONTHS' CLOTHING.		BOUNTY FOR RE-ENLISTING.		COMMUTATION IN LIEU OF TRANSPORTATION FOR RE-ENLISTING.		TOTAL AMOUNT DUE.		AMOUNT OF STOPPAGES.		BALANCE PAID.		RECEIVED PAYMENT OF—	WITNESS.
Mos.	Days.	Dolls.	Dolls.	Cts.	Dolls.	Cts.	Dolls.	Cts.	Dolls.	Cts.	Dolls.	Cts.	Dolls.	Cts.	Dolls.	Cts.		
8	16	17	145	06							145	06					Wm Bandy	F. M. Holstead Capt
2		17	34	00							34	00					N. Burgess	"
11	24	17	200	60							200	60					William Harris	"
2		17	34	00							34	00					S. C. Sawyer	"
10	21	13	139	10							139	10					Charles Burfoot	F. M. Holstead
2		13	26	00							26	00					Eagar B. Gilliam	"
2		13	26	00							26	00					Willoughby Gregory	"
2		13	26	00							26	00					Joseph H. Stirling	"
2		11	22	00							22	00					Jas. E. Abell	F. M. Holstead
10	21	11	117	70							117	70					Baily Barco	F. M. Holstead
1	29	11	28	63							28	63					Luther Coffey	F. M. Holstead
2		11	22	00							22	00					George Cartwright	"
2		11	22	00							22	00					G. S. Edwards	"
2		11	22	00							22	00					John Etheridge	"
2	26	11	31	53							31	53					B. M. Ellis	F. M. Holstead
2		11	22	00							22	00					George Earnhart	"
2		11	22	00							22	00					Henry Earnhart	"
2		11	22	00							22	00					John Foster	"
2		11	22	00							22	00					Kenneth R. Gallop	F. M. Holstead
11	24	11	129	80							129	80					Major D. Gregory	F. M. Holstead
1	29	11	21	63							21	63					Jas. Gammon	"
2		11	22	00							22	00					Thos. Jones	F. M. Holstead
2	26	11	31	53							31	53					George Keek	"
2		11	22	00							22	00					Andrew Keek	"
2		11	22	00							22	00					Hilory R. Land	"
11	26	11	129	80							129	80					E. S. Lamb	"
8		11	88	00							88	00					Chs. B. Morisette	F. M. Holst.
2																	Richard Roberts	F. M. Holst.
2																	Samuel Savalls	"
2																	Peter B. Smith	"
2																	Malichi Smith	"

William N. Elliott

Photo circa 1862

A
TARHEEL
CONFEDERATE
AND
HIS FAMILY

BY HIS GRANDSON
ROBERT GARRISON ELLIOTT

Robert G. Elliott

A TARHEEL CONFEDERATE and HIS FAMILY

First Edition

Library of Congress Catalog Card Number 89-61337

Published 1989 by
R. G. E. PUBLICATIONS
P. O. Box 9281
Daytona Beach, Fl, 32020

ISBN 0-9622799-0-0

Manufactured by
Rose Printing Company, Inc.
2503 Jackson Bluff Rd.
P.O. Box 5078
Tallahassee, Fl, 32314

CONTENTS

Preface   xii

THE YEARS BEFORE THE WAR   1

1861 - 1862   7

1863   16

1864   39

1865   63

HE BEGINS ANEW   73

AMBITIONS REALIZED   87

A VETERAN RECOGNIZED   107

Bibliography   125

Index   127

ILLUSTRATED

DEDICATION

I dedicate this book, as a salute, to a veteran
of the Confederate Army. He was my grandfather,
Lt. William Harrison Elliott, who, with honor,
served the Cause.

It is my hope that the younger and older relatives of grandfather William, will cherish this
link in their heritage. When the last page has
been turned, may they retain a sense of having
known him,...just a little.

FOREWORD

" To speak the name of the dead, is to make him
live again. "

So spake the ancient Egyptians who believed that speaking the name of the departed, brought back to life, one who had departed this earth.

Bob Elliott's quest for the history of his family, particularly that of his grandfather, William Harrison Elliott, has taken him literally in those paths this young Confederate officer walked so dangerously. Bob has not only made him live again, but has lived, with him.

The courageous fight Company B of the 68th North Carolina waged against Northern aggression is an epic tale. They were not waging a war of aggression, but were fighting for their homeland and their hearthstones.

Striking with suddenness against the pillaging negro soldiers, they could just as quickly retreat into their swampland fastness that they knew so well. The baffling water wastelands were a sanctuary that was impenetrable to the Northern invaders until their eventual withdrawal.

The chance discovery of the Muster Roll of these fine Confederate soldiers has inscribed their names in the history of the Cause as it was lived in North Carolina.

It is a great tribute to Robert G. Elliott's perseverance, in telling this story of his grandfather. The thrill and satisfaction of walking with his grandfather in the very paths in which he made history, is the experience that few men know. For his fine story, I commend Bob to his peers.

Frank G. Rankin, Jr., Historian General
Military Order of the Stars and Bars

ACKNOWLEDGEMENTS

I have undertaken this study of my grandfather's life for deep-felt personal reasons. One quickly learns, however, that whatever is to be achieved, depends greatly upon the support of others.

Early on, my family expressed interest in my research, and contributed information long stored in their memory. When it came time to establish where grandfather's parents lived, only one individual knew. Once aware of my project, my good friend, William W. Forehand, historian of Camden County, North Carolina, rose to the occasion. He gave me maps. He told me of the ancestral properties. Together, we walked upon those parcels of land.

My cousin, Dorothy M. Pritchard, of Elizabeth City, has repeatedly answered my calls for additional bits of information, available only from civil and private sources, where she lives.

Encouragement also was received from Frank G. Rankin, of Louisville, Kentucky. A noted Kentucky historian, Frank was captivated with the scope of my undertaking, as he, too, has Confederate Army ancestors. He has written the "FOREWORD."

For his editorial recommendations, I thank my friend, Ralph W. Widener, Jr., of Dallas, Texas. He, too, is a descendant of a Confederate veteran.

Jerrold Northrop Moore, of Worcestershire, England, an accomplished author, willingly offered his views as a literary critic. Jerrold shares my desire to portray the life of my Confederate veteran grandfather. His great-great uncle was General Lucius B. Northrop, Commissary General of the Confederacy.

Most prominent through it all has been the firm support of my wife, Muriel.

PREFACE

Who has not, at one time or another, wondered about an ancestor one was never privileged to know? Was he a pleasing personality? What was his trade or profession? What did he look like? Where did he live? With whom?

My grandfather, William Harrison Elliott, suffered a final illness, at home, near Nixonton, North Carolina. He died, on January 21, 1914. That was five years and three months before I was born. I first became aware of him during my early growing-up years. His name had occasionally been mentioned by my dad, while he reminisced of North Carolina. We were living in central New York state. Being only a little boy, unaware of geography, North Carolina seemed like an unknown place, far far away. Were it not for my parents' numerous photo albums, it might have been years later before I became very knowledgeable of my Carolina folks.

Interest in dad's North Carolina family came into sharp focus, in 1973-1974, when I began a serious genealogical study of my Elliott roots. Vaguely, I recalled the family mentioning that grandfather had been a soldier in the Confederate Army. I learned, too, of the Sons of Confederate Veterans, and wanted to join. To do so, I needed proof of his service. I had little, but hoped for more.

In retrospect, I realized the family had spoken very little of his military service. Why was this? Would not my dad have known something about grandfather's army life? Didn't he ask? Wouldn't grandfather tell him? Who knew?

My aunts and uncle never said much, unless encouraged. But they too, knew little. For several years before she died, my grandmother Elliott spent her winters with us. My mother often jotted down what grandmother said, by using pen and ink in small note books. Years later, when I finally had them to read, I learned there was little evidence of grandfather's army experience.

By 1974, it was obvious that I had to learn something of what had happened, fifty-eight years before I was born. In sorting through boxes of old family letters, I came upon one letter, written by my mother, in 1936, to Billy and Harriett Elliott. They were the children of dad's deceased brother, Bill. The letter has been returned by the post office, stamped "Undeliverable." What struck me like a bolt was her question to them, "Did you know what ever became of grandfather's sword?" She then said, "I've just learned how grandfather was awarded his sword, did you ever know?" Mother made no further mention of where she learned about the sword. Was it a trophy of war, or was it 'awarded' him as an officer?

A cousin from the Elliott-Newbold line, described to me, what seems to have been the (very) last act of my grandfather's life. The tale (first told to her by an older lady in the Newbold family) had to do with the delirium from grandfather's final illness.

Confined to bed, he suddenly roused from apparent slumber. Wild-eyed, he scrambled from bed. Steps away was the fireplace hearth. Standing there was the fireplace poker. Grasping it fiercely, and waving it high, he dashed about the room, shouting, "Charge, Charge."

I wonder if this really happened? How long was it before he died? Who saw him do this?

The same cousin also said he had a Commission. It was thought to be stored away somewhere in a box of her family records. I wonder if either of these tales will ever become fact?

At the time my research was underway, my father, Joseph Keaton Elliott, met me in Elizabeth City, North Carolina. For several days we drove over the country roads of Camden and Pasquotank counties. My tape recorder, on the car seat, preserved his reminiscences. We stopped at each location he remembered, from those days as a child, to early manhood.

Knowledge of my grandfather William's early life, especially his Confederate Army service, was almost subliminal. I now had a tantalizing array of questions. Pursuit of each could bring an answer. Logically, I decided to start with his parents. From there his life would unfold. What follows is my impression of those events that molded his life, influenced his personality, and formed his character.

Robert G. Elliott

THE YEARS BEFORE THE WAR

My grandfather was a North Carolinian from Colonial stock. From the beginning of the 18th Century, his mother's family, the Brockett's, were residents of Pasquotank County, in extreme northeastern North Carolina. The area where they lived, near Shiloh, became part of newly-formed Camden County. Camden was formed after breaking away from Pasquotank County in 1777. [1]

Grandfather's paternal grandfather, Peter Elliott, had lived in Virginia. He was married in Norfolk, on October 8, 1790. The bride was Tamar Burgess, a native of Camden County. [2] Within the second decade of the 1800's, they had moved to North Carolina. Their first home was in the vicinity of the 'float bridge,' near Elizabeth City.

Peter became engaged in various business ventures. Subsequently, he owned numerous parcels of land in Elizabeth City. One parcel, in particular, he purchased from Revolutionary War hero, General Peter Dauge, for the sum of $200.00. The date of purchase was June 2, 1817. [3] Before the year was up, he had sold his land, known as 'Elliott's Wharf,' on the Pasquotank River, for $600.00. [4]

Four years later, on April 1, 1821, Peter Elliott died in Elizabeth City. [5]

Peter left his widow, Tamar Burgess Elliott, and his three sons, Gilbert, Peter, and William. Within eight years Tamar Elliott had died, in Elizabeth City, during the first week of October, 1829. She was 67. [6] Peter and Tamar Elliott's son, Peter, would later be my great grandfather. This young man, Peter, was living in Camden County by 1825. What may have been one of his first land acquisitions occurred, on November 12, 1825. For $314.00, he purchased about forty acres of land near Shiloh. [7] On February 14, 1826, Peter was

Notes:

1. Three Hundred Years Along the Pasquotank, by Jesse Pugh
2. Marriages of Norfolk County,VA.,1706-1792,Vol.I,pg.22,by Wingo
3. Pasquotank Deed Book, V, pgs. 15, 16, 17
4. Pasquotank Deed Book, 1817-1820, pg. 102
5. The American Beacon Daily, Norfolk, Va., April 6, 1821
6. The Raleigh Register, October 8, 1829
7. Camden Deed Book, T, pg. 126

appointed the first Postmaster of Shiloh. His first annual pay was $3.73.[1] He held this position, until March 31, 1830.

My grandfather William's parents, Peter Elliott and Mary Brockett Elliott, were married and living in Camden County, by late 1839.[2]

Peter's age was between 30 and 40 by 1840. Mary Brockett was born near Shiloh, in Camden County, on February 29, 1812. A son, their first child, was born on February 13, 1841. They named him William Harrison Elliott.[3]

The search for Peter's property transactions began in the Camden Court House. My findings were compared with many detailed records of early Shiloh family properties, provided by William W. Forehand, of Shiloh. We located, with a satisfactory degree of accuracy, the many parcels lived on by Peter, his wife Mary, their son William H., and their daughter, Mary Jane. These represented a span of years, running from 1839, to the mid-1870's. The map on page 4 identifies a number of these farm and residence sites.

Today, there are two houses in Shiloh that were early occupied by Peter and Mary Elliott.[4] In all probability Peter, with his wife and son, was living in the house a short distance west of the Shiloh Church in 1841. (see Fig. 3, page 4)

The second child born to Peter and Mary Elliott was a second son. Born on February 8, 1843, they named him Charles T. Elliott.[5] Two pages from an old family record appear on page 6. Since the Elliott's and Tillett's lived on adjoining lands in 1842,[6] the two families may have developed a close friendship. I sense this by the fact that Samuel Tillett was visiting Mary B. Elliott in 1850, when the Camden Census was recorded. In later years, he also purchased farm land from Mary to lighten her financial burden. I believe that son Charles'

Notes:

1. Three Hundred Years Along the Pasquotank, by J. Pugh, pg. 170
2. 1840 Camden Census
3. Elliott family Bible, Nancy Elliott (Mrs. John P. Elliott, Jr.),
   Richmond, Va., & Joseph K. Elliott's birth cert., author's property
4. William W. Forehand's personal collection at Shiloh
5. Family Bible, Eula Newbold Greenwood, Kittrell, N. C.
6. Deed Book, X, pg. 245, Camden County Court House

Extensively remodeled over the years, a portion of this house west of the Shiloh Church, was the residence of Peter Elliott, and his wife, Mary Brockett Elliott, in 1839. His little store was located a few hundred feet west. The small structure in the rear easily dates to the same period and was used as servants quarters and cook-house. (See Fig. 3 on map, page 4)

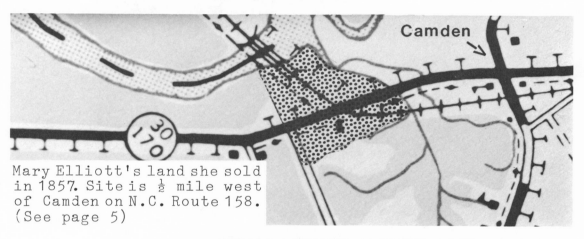

Mary Elliott's land she sold in 1857. Site is ½ mile west of Camden on N.C. Route 158. (See page 5)

Peter's final house east of the village had been a portion of Jonathan Brockett's farm. In recent times it was occupied by Dr. Elizabeth McPherson, a retired historian. The house is nearly original. (See Fig. 4 on map, page 4)

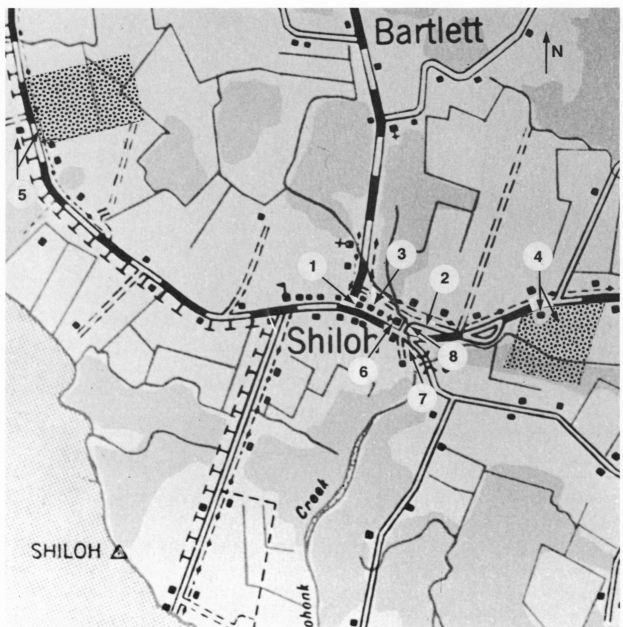

Bartlett

N

Shiloh

SHILOH △

Creek

Texaco Beach

1. Peter Elliott, store/post office, 1827.
2. Peter Elliott and wife, Meddy, owned this property in the early 1830's.
3. Peter Elliott residence, March 8, 1839.
4. Peter Elliott, wife Mary Brockett, and children residence about 1841-47.
5. Farm of Joseph Walston and bride, Mary Jane Elliott.
6. Shiloh Baptist Church.
7. Present cemetery.
8. Old cemetery, probably disturbed.

middle initial, 'T', may have represented the name Tillett. It is said that Charles died in an accident shortly after the 1850 Census, when a load of wood fell upon him.

Peter was very active buying and selling land. He also owned a small store within walking distance of his home. The date of Peter's death is not recorded, but he had died before the year's end in 1846.

My grandfather's sister, Mary Jane ('Mollie'), was born on January 14, 1845.[1] She later married Joseph S. Walston, on December 14, 1871. Joseph Walston's farm was in the immediate vicinity of Shiloh, though somewhat northwest, on the main road, towards the village of Camden. Mary and her husband, Joseph, are buried in the graveyard adjacent to the Shiloh Baptist Church, and have headstones. In later years, just prior to her death, on July 7, 1885, Mary Brockett Elliott lived with her daughter Mollie, and Joseph Walston. After her death, Mary B. Elliott could very well have been buried in the same Shiloh cemetery. An older section of the church burial ground, just north and on the east side of the structure, may have also been the burial site of Peter Elliott. We cannot be positive of this, however, as the cemetery was disturbed when the highway was reconstructed.

William's mother, Mary, continued to buy and sell land after the death of Peter. From September 12, 1845, to November 14, 1857, Mary's signature appears on six property transactions. On November 7, 1846, she sold the farm they had lived on when Peter died. For the 70 acre property, she received $1,100.00, from William Bartlett.[2] Four years later, Mary B. Elliott was listed as head of household, on the 1850 Census.

The next purchase she made was on October 22, 1849. Mary paid Willis Etheridge $1,000.00 for sixty-seven acres.[3]

Mary B. Elliott bought ten additional acres from Samuel Upton, on April 29, 1852, for which she paid $100.00 [4]

Notes:

1. Family Bible, Eula Newbold Greenwood, Kittrell, N. C.
2. Camden Deed Book, BB, pgs. 61, 62
3. Camden Deed Book, Z, pg. 106
4. Camden Deed Book, AA, pg. 418

These two purchases constituted the property represented by the shaded area of the map on page 3.

Mary sold this farm, just west of the village of Camden, on November 14, 1857. For the seventy-seven acres, she received $1,450.00 from Samuel B. Tillett.[1]

Sometime after 1857, Mary, with William and Mary Jane, moved to the vicinity of Elizabeth City, in Pasquotank County, a distance of about four miles west of the village of Camden. The fact that William's aunt, Sarah Grice Elliott, lived in Elizabeth City with her three sons, Charles Grice Elliott, Gilbert Elliott, and Warren Grice Elliott, may have been a direct incentive to settle there.[2]

Sarah's deceased husband, Gilbert Elliott, of Elizabeth City, had been a brother of William's father, Peter, in Shiloh. In three years, Mary B. Elliott, a resident of the Elizabeth City area, was known to be head of her house, and a seamstress. Her son, William, at age 19, was employed as a clerk, and her daughter, Mary Jane, was age 15.[3]

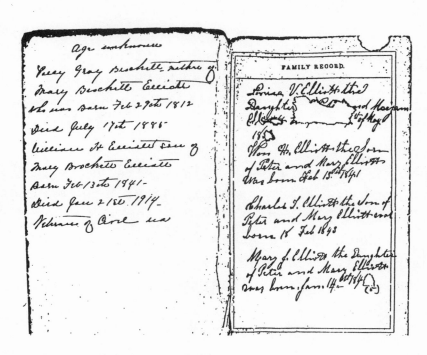

Notes:

1. Camden Deed Book, BB, pgs. 20, 21
2. 1860 Census, Pasquotank County, N. C.
3. 1860 Census, Pasquotank County, N. C.

1861 - 1862

During the ensuing year (1861), the Confederacy would have been born. North Carolina would have seceded from the Union.

The War had begun.

By mid-year in 1861, before General Ambrose Burnside's invasion of Hatteras Inlet, with the subsequent battle for Roanoke Island, elements of Union forces started filtering into northeastern North Carolina. They were advancing from the vicinity of Norfolk, Virginia. Their impending arrival caused much alarm and not a little apprehension among the citizens.

To counter this threat, the State of North Carolina very early sought responsible men to serve in State Guard units. Some select individuals were appointed as commissioned officers in the Confederate Army. They were to organize regional companies for protection against the invaders. The Union regarded the companies as partisan rangers, bandits, guerrillas, and rebels.

Although the organizations were commanded in a loose manner, with each Captain not being responsible to any formal command, they did, on occasion, assist each other. Governor Vance had issued orders, directing them to work together as military units, reporting to a common command, but to no avail. [1]

In those early months, the major concerns were to slash at the enemy, when opportunity presented itself. These encounters, caused great aggravation for the Federals. (continued page 12)

Note:
OR, Ser. I, Vol. XXIX, Pt. I, pg. 915

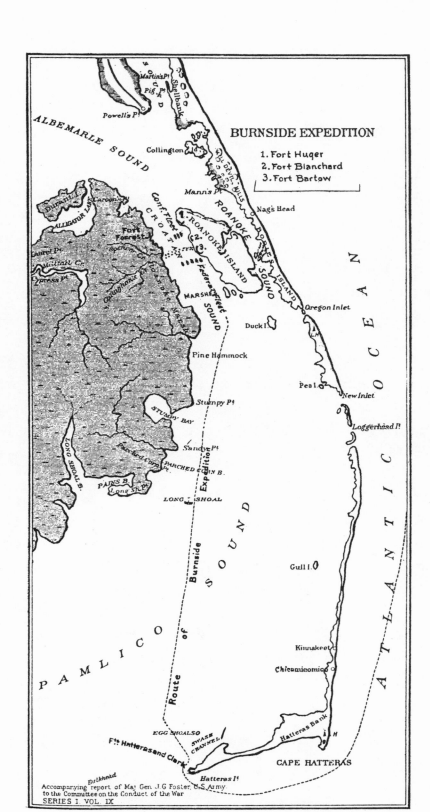

BURNSIDE EXPEDITION

1. Fort Huger
2. Fort Blanchard
3. Fort Bartow

Accompanying report of Maj. Gen. J. G. Foster, U.S. Army
to the Committee on the Conduct of the War
SERIES I. VOL. IX

LANDING OF TROOPS ON ROANOKE ISLAND.
BURNSIDE EXPEDITION.
AD 1862.

The above engraving of General Burnside's expedition depicts his sea-borne forces landing on Roanoke Island, during the first week of February, 1862.

It graphically portrays immensely superior Federal forces that were transported north in Croatan Sound, to their landing at Ashby Harbor, south of Fort Bartow.

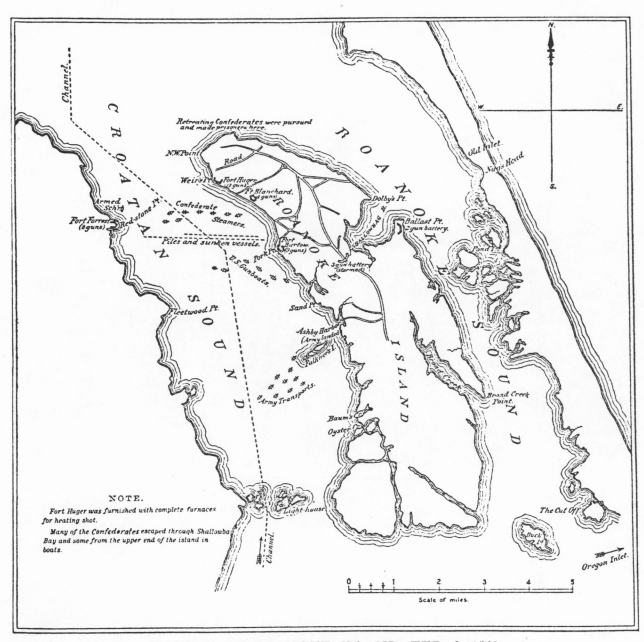

BATTLE OF ROANOKE ISLAND, FEB. 8, 1862.

Fort Bartow was the most southerly located of the three forts on Roanoke Island. By 7 AM, on February 8, 1862, Federal forces numbering 15,000 men were landing north of Ashby's Harbor, two miles south of Fort Bartow, and were making their way northward to attack the fort in it's rear. Colonel Henry M. Shaw, Senior Officer Commanding Confederate troops on the island, surrendered at the northern tip of the island later that day. The Roanoke Island defenders had been overwhelmed by superior forces of General Burnside's army.

Colonel Henry M. Shaw's home was built about 1797. The Colonel established residence in the early 1850's. Shawboro, the neighboring community, was named in his honor. Colonel Shaw was killed in the battle of New Bern, North Carolina, on February 1, 1864, with burial in a family plot near the house.

Silas Gregory, son of elderly Major Gregory who was captured and released, lived in this house. It's located between what was known as Sanderlin's swamp and Indiantown, in Camden County. Silas armed and fed the guerrilla troops in the vicinity. Although neighboring farms were burned, protection papers from Union General J. G. Foster prevented the destruction of Silas Gregory's house. (See text page 25)

In April and May, 1861, eleven companies were mustered, in the northeastern part of the State. They did not rendezvous to be mustered in a regiment, as was the usual practice, but were mustered separately, for twelve months service.

The news publishers were daily announcing events of the month-old war. Enlistment broadsides for the 17th Regiment could be seen prominently displayed in, and around, Elizabeth City. It's no wonder then, that the Elliott cousins each decided to enlist in Company L.

Enlistment in Company L, from Perquimans County, took place on May 4, 1861, in Elizabeth City.[1] In due course, brothers Charles Grice and Gilbert Elliott, with their cousin, William H. Elliott, were mustered into State service at Oregon Inlet, on July 28, 1861.[2]

On August 20, 1861, the group was transferred from State to Confederate service. They became components of the 17th Regiment, N.C. Volunteers. At the time of transfer, Companies A, C, D, E, F, G, and H, were stationed at Hatteras Inlet. Companies B and K were at Fort Ocracoke. Companies I and L were at Oregon Inlet, and were sent to Fort Bartow, on Roanoke Island. Their commander was Major Gabriel H. Hill.

That fall, on November 14, 1861, the Adjutant and Inspector-General's Office at Richmond, issued Special Order 222. It designated them as the 17th Regiment, N.C. Troops (7th Regiment, N.C. Volunteers.)[3]

At Fort Bartow, Company L served the two 32 pounders on Barbette. The Barbette was a huge mound of earth upon which a large gun was emplaced. At 11 AM, on February 7, 1862, the Federal forces of General Ambrose Burnside, began shelling the fort from their ships in the sound. At noon, a shell exploded on the Barbette, causing several casualties. Members of Company L also manned similar guns in embrasures with respectable results. Embrasures were narrow slots,

Notes:

1. N.C.Troops, 1861-1865, by Weymouth T.Jordan,Jr.,Vol. VI, pg. 191
2. N.C.Troops, 1861-1865, by Weymouth T.Jordan,Jr.,Vol. VI, pg. 191
3. N.C.Troops, 1861-1865, by Weymouth T.Jordan,Jr.,Vol. VI, pg. 118

with flaring sides, located in the fortress walls.

At 4 AM, on the 8th, the company was roused in the rain. By 7 AM the cannonading began, and lasted until 10 AM. At noon, Major Hill received a dispatch from Colonel Shaw, informing him of the Confederate retreat. A Federal force of 15,000 men had landed, and were advancing toward their rear. Major Hill ordered the 100-man Battery to disable the guns. Then, in perfect order, they marched to Colonel Shaw's headquarters. Their expectations of assignment to Fort Huger, to the north, were shattered, when they were surrendered as prisoners-of-war.

After waiting in camp for two weeks, the prisoners were removed to Elizabeth City, where they were paroled, on February 21. Their exchange was then awaited at home. After the regiment was disbanded in March, 1862, the men were still on parole. Their exchange came in August, five months later. All troops were then mustered out of service.[1] Reviewing portions of Company L's roster, I have noted a 2nd Lt. Charles Gilbert Elliott. The 'Gilbert' is an error. Charles' middle name was 'Grice.'[2] Younger Gilbert had no middle initial. He was in the 17th Regiment (First Organization), and later was a 1st Lt., and Adjutant, of the 17th Regiment (Second Organization).[3] Charles Grice Elliott, after his exchange, was appointed Captain, A. A. G. (Assistant Adjutant General), of the Martin-Kirkland Brigade.[4] Private William H. Elliott, in the same roster, is noted as a resident of Pasquotank County. He had been a clerk, and had enlisted in Elizabeth City at the age of 20, on May 4, 1861. He was present and accounted for, until captured at Roanoke Island, on February 8, 1862. He was paroled in Elizabeth City, on February 21, 1862, and exchanged in August of the same year. He was present and accounted for when the company disbanded, around March 4, 1863.[5]

Notes:
1. OR, Ser. I, Vol. IX, pgs. 170-191
2. Parish of Christ Church records, Elizabeth City, pgs. 85, 185, 188
3. N. C. Troops, 1861-1865, by Weymouth T. Jordan, Jr., Vol. VI, pg. 204
4. N. C. Regiments, 1861-1865, by Walter Clark, Vol. IV, pg. 527
5. N. C. Troops, 1861-1865, by Weymouth T. Jordan, Jr., Vol. VI, pg. 195

After William was exchanged in August, 1862, he renewed former friendships. While doing so, he learned of another resistance unit being formed in adjacent, and occupied, Camden County. Residents of counties bordering on the northern shores of Albemarle Sound, had been living under the shadow of Union occupation, since mid-summer of 1861. In Camden County, there was Captain Willis B. Sanderlin, who commanded one of these shadowy partisan units.

Concurrent with General Ambrose Burnside's attack upon Roanoke Island, elements of Union forces were encountered in the counties of Currituck, Camden, Pasquotank, and Perquimans, all bordering on the northern shores of Albemarle Sound.

On February 10, 1862, Colonel E. C. Henningsen, commanding artillery of General Wise's Legion, submitted a lengthy and detailed report covering all his encounters with the enemy, in and around, Elizabeth City. Although Colonel Henningsen succeeded in:

> "placing batteries to guard the river approaches, Federal steamers...rapidly approaching,..forced his withdrawal by the old Edenton road,..where a halt was called for the night at Newby's Bridge, two miles from Hertford. The next day,...a small party of..artillery soldiers,...with teams, were sent back to Elizabeth City to salvage..a wagon and caisson, which had been left concealed a mile southwest of town." 1

There can be little doubt that residents of the area were well informed of this activity. In particular would be those recently-paroled troops from Roanoke Island. Tensions continued to increase among the residents of Elizabeth City when:

> "at 4 AM, on April 8, 1862, 600 men on board Federal steamers Virginia, Putnam, Ceres and Eagle were landed. Two companies of the New York Ninth entered the city,...while four companies of the New Hampshire Sixth worked..their way north for six miles from the city. In this..sweeping maneuver they pursued and captured 73 troops of the First Brigade, North Carolina Militia." 2

Notes:

1. OR, Ser. I, Vol. IX, pg. 191
2. OR, Ser. I, Vol. IX, pg. 296

In that skirmish, a scout, Tim Gregory, was shot, and a vedette wounded. Had they not been on parole, those former Roanoke Island defenders would indeed, have been in personal jeopardy under this Federal occupation. [1]

Militia troops, operating in Camden County, attacked a Federal force that had landed six miles south of Shiloh, during the night of September 17, 1862. Federal Captain E. C. Sanders, First North Carolina Infantry, sent his report to Colonel W. A. Howard, acknowledging that:

> "while a majority of his force was in Elizabeth City that night, the Militia..surprised the encampment killing 3 men, wounding 3, with 5 or 6 taken prisoner, in addition..to all arms, ammunition, stores, and provisions being taken."

Further on, in Captain Sander's report to Colonel Howard, reference was made to an event which occurred on Friday, September 9, at 4 PM:

> "Captain William B. Avery, commander of the U.S. gunboat, Lancer, responding to an urgent summons, arrived at Shiloh with 60 men. At 9:30 PM they departed for the last known location of the Militia troops, to learn...that the rebels were about four miles away in a swamp near the 'lake'. His men pursued in carts, while others were on foot, often changing places,..thus causing little fatigue on the 12 mile march. In time, the Militia was spotted, but quickly disappeared in a swamp. A howitzer, which was said...to have been hidden on the swamp, was never found. Footsore and exhausted, the men arrived back in Shiloh that night about 6:30 PM, having been gone about 24 hours. By 8 PM all were once more on board the Lancer."[2]

Notes:
1. OR, Ser. I, Vol. IX, pg. 296
2. OR, Ser. I, Vol. XVIII, pg. 13

1863

At Nixonton, along the Little River, grandfather would one day
live on his farm, only a mile north. An incident occurred there, on
April 6, 1863. In his descriptive report, dated May 1, 1863, Captain E. C. Sanders related events of another expedition to Pasquotank County, arriving by sea. At 5 AM, on April 4, Captain Sanders,
with a company of infantry, boarded the Union gunboat, Southfield,
at Plymouth, on the southwest shore of Albemarle Sound.

(If one could have peered into the future, one would have known
that, on April 18, 1864, the Southfield would be sunk near Plymouth,
during an encounter with the CSS Ram Albemarle. The Albemarle was
built by grandfather's cousin, 1st Lt. Gilbert Elliott, former Adjutant of the 17th Regiment's second organization. Gilbert had been
commissioned for the project by Stephen R. Mallory, Secretary of the
Confederate Navy).

In the report of his voyage across Albemarle Sound, Captain Sanders noted that:

> "landfall..on..the..opposite..shore at Halley's
> Landing..occurred at 9 AM, though the wharf had
> been burned by the Confederates. Initial inquery
> determined that rebel Company E (Captain John T.
> Elliott's,..no relation to William H.), was en-
> camped..in the woods,..ten miles..distant,..and
> because of..my uncertainty,..I thought..it..not
> prudent to penetrate..the countryside. By 5 PM,
> our voyage..brought us to the Pasquotank River-
> mouth, where we landed and marched ten miles to
> Shiloh, then at 10 PM re-boarded the gunboat"..

which had steamed to an anchorage, just west of Shiloh, in the Pasquotank River:

> "next morning on the 5th, we proceeded to Eliz-
> abeth City..and..'got..the family..of...William
> Wright,' then back to Shiloh, noting the arrival
> of a schooner, the Patty Martin. Continuing by
> boat to Jones' Mill,..we landed..and marched to

Notes:

1.N. C. Regiments, 1861-1865, by Walter Clark, pg. 320
2.N. C. Regiments, 1861-1865, by Walter Clark, pgs. 315-323

Old Trap, found some of the men collected there
but..the others,..not knowing of..our presence,
could not be found. At daylight, I and..7 of my
men..(Peter,..Stephen,..Cornelius, and Nicholas
Burgess, Ithean (Ithrum) and Wilson Duncan, and
Dempsey Wright) went on board..and crossed over
to the Pasquotank side."

Obviously, these men, and others collected, were Union sympathizers. The first 'rescue,' was:

"the family of Joseph Morgan. Of four men from
my company..in Pasquotank,..John Cartwright was
located, one was missing and two were, one sick
and one wounded. We went aboard at dark. At daylight on..the 6th..I started for Nixonton,...on
Little River, in the schooner Patty Martin with
17 men....We arrived..and anchored..at 5 PM off
Thomas Moss' landing,..sent a small boat with 6
men with orders..(to..reconnoiter before..going
ashore)...Approaching the land they saw a hand-
kerchief..waved in..the window..of Mrs. Moss'..
house. Putting about and pulling for the schooner, they were fired upon by the guerrillas."

Both the small boat, and schooner, returned fire until the small
boat was taken aboard, whereupon the schooner sailed down the river.
At sunset they met the Union steamer, Whitehead. Next morning, on
returning to Nixonton, they got the Moss family and sailed for Roanoke Island. In all, Sanders left 11 men in Camden, 3 in Pasquotank,
and 2 in Elizabeth City, all of whom were in hiding and had not been
notified of the rescue attempt. [1]

Major J. W. Wallis, Union Post Commander at Elizabeth City, in
his April, 1863, report to AAG Hoffman, Headquarters, remarked about
Captain Sanders' 17-man expedition, adding that:

"those men went ashore after dark..to see their
families and were surprised..by the guerrillas,
taken prisoner, and returned to Richmond,..thus
leaving 14 men for duty."

Note:
1.OR, Ser. I, Vol. XVIII, pg. 259

Major Wallis urgently requested a company of cavalry to rout out the guerrilla force. Indeed, he registered a plea for rations, with comment that, "foraging from the citizens was becoming too expensive, when compared to government provisions from New Bern." [1]

By the middle of May, the occupation forces again felt the sting from the valiant guerrilla defenders. Captain F. E. Porter, Post Commander, Eighth Massachusetts Infantry, reported to Brig. General H. W. Wessells, that the Union steamers, Emily and Arrow, were captured by partisans at Currituck Sound, on May 15, 1863.

General Wessells' endorsed report for Headquarters, on May 17, stated one hundred fifty infantry were embarking to attempt the recapture or destruction of the Emily and Arrow. [2]

A report of Captain E. Dewees Roberts, Eleventh Pennsylvania Vol. Cavalry, dated May 17, from Camden Court House, and Shiloh, began:

> "Major: I have the honor..to make the following report from..the expedition sent out..yesterday afternoon,..to intercept..the party supposed to have captured..the Emily and Arrow. The..Pasquotank guerrillas crossed the Pasquotank River about five miles below Elizabeth City on Friday morning, the 15th. About 4 PM they captured one of the above named boats in Currituck Canal, and with her, pushed out into North River where they captured the other vessel, taking all crew members prisoner. They then landed..the prisoners and,..under sufficient guard,..took them across the lower end of Camden County..to near Shiloh, then across..the Pasquotank River..to Elizabeth City,..where they arrived on the morning of the 16th. Hearing of a Federal force in the vicinity under..Lt. Titus,..they again went..down river, landing on the south shore. Both captured boats seem..to have been..taken down..Albemarle Sound

Notes:
1. OR, Ser. I, Vol. XVIII, pg. 675
2. OR, Ser. I, Vol. XVIII, pg. 355

and up the Chowan River. The rebel crew had de-
clared this to be their intention, but, if over-
taken by our forces they would destroy the ships.
(Capturing..these boats..was accomplished..by a
party) of some 40 Pasquotank guerrillas,..Capt.
(John T.) Elliott, commanding, while being guid-
ed by..Captain Sanderlin,..of the..Camden guerrillas. None..of the Camden company, except the
Captain, were engaged in the capture."

Major Franklin A. Stratton, Eleventh Pennsylvania Cavalry, Det.
at South Mills wrote, on May 17, to General Viele at Headquarters,
that indeed, Captain Roberts was provided with the company of cavalry, and a howitzer, to effect the interception, but their arrival
was too late. Lt. Titus' company, at Elizabeth City, may have caused the ship captors to hurry away down river to the Sound. [1]

Every army of occupation has attempted to suppress civilians by
acts of depredation. Not only were crops, livestock, and personal
property confiscated, but also Federal wrath was directed at civilians themselves. One particular incident was most starkly illumi-
nated in a report, released in mid-February, 1864, by a special committee to inquire into certain outrages committed in December, 1863,
by Union troops, against Pasquotank citizens. Such a committee was
assigned this task, by the House of Representatives in Raleigh.

A synopsis of subjects addressed, were the depredations of Brig.
General Edward A. Wild, commanding all negro soldiers, who occupied
Camden and Pasquotank counties. A citizen, Daniel Bright, was hung,
by the roadside, just north of Elizabeth City. Bright was a former
soldier of the 62nd Georgia Regiment, with authority of Governor
Vance, to raise a company in Pasquotank for local defense. During
a brief skirmish, the committee noted that a small Confederate force
captured two of General Wild's negro soldiers, and for this outrage,
General Wild broke the laws of civilized war, by arresting two ladies.
Under orders from Major General Pickett, on January 12, 1864, one

Note:
1.OR, Ser. I, Vol. XVIII, pg. 356

of the two captured soldiers, Private Samuel Jordan, Co. B, Fifth Ohio Regiment, was hung as reprisal for the hanging of Daniel Bright.

Federal retaliation was directed against Mrs. Elizabeth Weeks, wife of Private Pender Weeks, and Mrs. Phoebe Munden, wife of Lt. W. J. Munden, of Captain John T. Elliott's company. Both were taken as hostage, abused, humiliated, and physically mistreated in public, then taken to Norfolk for imprisonment. Dwellings in both counties were also burned, among them were those of Captain Willis Sanderlin, and Major Gregory. An aged gentleman of 70 years, Gregory, was taken hostage, all his properties burned, and while a prisoner, he suffered a seizure which caused his release. Returned to friends, he endured great pain, dying a few days later.

The committee acknowledged the companies of Captains Willis B. Sanderlin and John T. Elliott, Co. E, had been legally raised in their counties by order of the Governor. These officers were commissioned by the State, and had been in service for well over a year. Their original attachment was to the Sixty-Sixth North Carolina Regiment, under command of Colonel James W. Hinton.

There does not appear to be a record of the committee's conclusion, in their examination of this matter. [1]

Meager Confederate defensive forces, coupled with insufficient arms and provisions, matched against the Union industrial machine, would, had the truth been known, portend the future.

William and his friends, during this unsettled period, were quietly waiting for a turn of events which would allow them to again confront the enemy. This interest was kept most confidential, due to the Federal occupation, but by word of mouth, they learned when to meet somewhere in Shiloh, where a company was being raised.

Note:
1.OR, Ser. II, Vol. VI, pgs. 1127-1129

The meeting, which would result in his second enlistment, was on June 6, 1863. In total, 51 signatures were afixed to the official muster roll. Captain Willis B. Sanderlin signed as Mustering Officer, on July 7, 1863, for three years or the war.

The company, without designation of regiment, would, after the last day of December that year, be known as Co. B, Sixty-Eighth Regiment, North Carolina Troops. Regimental Commander was Colonel James W. Hinton, from Pasquotank County, who was commissioned on July 8, 1863.[1] In June, Colonel Hinton's 68th was at Weldon. The District was commanded by General L. S. Baker, with headquarters at Goldsboro.[2]

Original officers of Co. B, of the 68th were: Captain Willis B. Sanderlin; 1st Lt. F. M. Halstead; 2nd Lt's Enoch Stevens and Willis W. Morrisette. The non-commissioned officer was: 1st Sgt. T. L. Morrisette who later died in prison at Point Lookout, Maryland, on January 6, 1864.[3]

This company was one of four to be raised in occupied territory (northeastern North Carolina). Though never a formal regiment of the Confederate States Army, the 68th was designed solely as a Home Guard force, to assist wherever needed within the State.[4]

One month after grandfather William had reenlisted near Shiloh, Captain W. Dewees Roberts, Eleventh Pennsylvania Volunteer Cavalry, in a report to Captain George H. Johnston, AAG, under General Wild, spoke of late activities near Camden Court House when he was fired upon by an estimated 20 guerrillas. Roberts perceived that:

> "there..to be four companies..of guerrillas..in
> the area. One in Camden, one in Pasquotank with
> headquarters..in a swamp..near..Elizabeth City,
> one in Perquimans and the fourth near Edenton,"

all belonging to the Sixty-Sixth North Carolina Regiment.[5]

Notes:

1. N.C.Troops, by John W. Moore, Vol. IV, pg. 147
2. N.C.Regiments, 1861-1865, by Walter Clark, Vol. IV, pg. 11
3. N.C.Regiments, 1861-1865, by Walter Clark, Vol. III, pg. 713
4. N.C.Regiments, 1861-1865, by Walter Clark, Vol. V, pg. 6
5. OR, Ser. I, Vol. XXIX, Pt. I, pgs. 30,31

This is a reduced composite copy of the original Muster of Captain Sanderlin's Camden Company. The original is a two-sided document.

William H. Elliott was the fourth enlistee in Sanderlin's Camden Company.

MUSTER ROLL of Captain Willis B. Sanderlin, Company B

		Age
Willis B. Sanderlin	Captain	32
Simeon Burgess	1st Lt.	28
Enoch Stevens	2nd Lt.	27
W. W. Morrisette	2nd Lt.	24
T. L. Morrisette	1st Sgt.	32

		Age			Age
Christopher Bray	Private	40	Joseph Stevens	Private	18
George Cartwright	"	26	Marshall Sawyer	"	23
William H. Elliott	"	24	Thomas Sikes	"	30
John Flora	"	25	Samuel Savills	"	24
Blucher Fletcher	"	19	Charles Taylor	"	18
John Foster	"	22	John B. Tillett	"	33
Keneth Galop	"	19	John B. Taylor	"	28
Major D. Gregory	"	19	George T. Throp	"	21
Edgar Gilbert	"	19	Samuel Whitehurst	"	20
Thomas Gordon	"	25	John Wright	"	18
Marshall Hughes	"	18	John Griffin	"	22
Job Hughes	"	19	Francis Ewell	"	22
William Harris	"	22	Cason Gregory	"	30
Edward Ives	"	55	Nathan Sawyer	"	20
Andrew Jackson	"	21	Thomas L. Garrett	"	20
Felix Jones	"	22	Peter B. Smith	"	17
Hilory Land	"	22	Bailey Barco	"	19
Thomas D. Mercer	"	35	Caleb G. Everton	"	21
Almon Morris	"	25	Joseph E. Parr	"	22
Samuel D. Morrisette	"	23	Thomas Jones	"	22
John Perkins	"	19	George L. Brown	"	18
Levi Perkins	"	19	Miles Jones	"	23
John D. Pool	"	18	Cary Brown	"	20

" I Certify on honor that I have mustered the men whose names are on this roll, and have accepted them in the service of the State of North Carolina for three years or the War from the 7th day of July, 1863. Willis B. Sanderlin, Mustering Officer."

An active presence of four companies increased Federal attention, as evidenced in Major General John J. Peck's report to Major General J. G. Foster, Commanding, Dept. of Virginia and North Carolina at New Bern. Dated October 10-17, 1863, it described a successful expedition to the counties north of Albemarle Sound. The Pasquotank company, under Colonel Hinton, was broken up and muster rolls captured. Enrolling officers of Perquimans and Chowan counties crossed the Chowan River in haste. General Peck believed that Union acceptance in that region was increasing, while occupants of Elizabeth City continued in a calm atmosphere, due to the Union 'friends.'

At this same time, excerpts from Captain William L. Kent's report, of October 17, 1863, to Colonel S. H. Mix, Third New York Cavalry, stated that the Twenty-Third Massachusetts Infantry Vols. with 100 men and 2 officers, sailed from New Bern at midnight, Saturday, October 10th. By 2 PM, on the 13th, they landed at Elizabeth City, where pickets were emplaced on all roads leading into town. On the Woodville Road, one artillery piece was positioned in a strategic manner. The next day Jack Heath, a notorious local guerrilla, was seen in the road for a brief moment. With his fleet horse, he escaped capture.

Taking advantage of the presence of Captain Kent's troops, Mr. Price, of Nixonton, 12 miles south of Elizabeth City, and Mr. G. W. Brooks, a resident on Body Road leading to Nixonton, were granted an audience with Captain Kent. They proposed to furnish a list of loyal Union citizens, a list of rebel sympathizers, the roster of Captain John T. Elliott's Co. E, located in a swamp near Parkville, as well as aiders and abettors. This meeting was accomplished with great personal risk. [1]

Note:
1. OR, Ser. I, Vol. XXIX, Pt. I, pgs. 477, 478

To stray for a moment, it's interesting to note that grandfather Elliott's third wife, Dorothy Keaton Price, was the widow of a Mr. John T. Price, in Nixonton. Dorothy's marriage to Mr. Price ended in 1886, when he died at home. Grandfather and his bride, Dorothy, purchased his Body Road farm, just one mile north of Nixonton, and settled there in early 1897. John T. Price was not among those mentioned as Union sympathizers.

Simultaneous with Captain Kent's landing at Elizabeth City, on October 13th, Lt. Colonel William Lewis, Fifth Pennsylvania Cavalry, reported to Acting AAG, Lt. C. H. Shepard, the results of his scouting foray:

> "to Indiantown Bridge by way of the great swamp road, a distance of seven miles. The advance on sighting the bridge,..observed a squad of 30 or 40 guerrillas on the bridge, however, they quickly took cover in the swampy woods,"

avoiding a confrontation with the Union cavalry, who had by then unlimbered a howitzer, and begun to shell the woods. After the brief exchange, the column proceeded:

> "three miles..beyond the bridge..to Major Gregory's house where they halted."

Scouts and pickets were sent out, as it was feared the guerrillas numbered about 300 men:

> "Twelve men under Lt. W. E. A. Bird were dispatched to arrest..Silas F. Gregory,..a notorious guerrilla,..but he had protection papers from Major General J. G. Foster, Commanding,...Department of Virginia and North Carolina."

Thus Silas F. Gregory's house escaped the torch. Silas Gregory was known to be:

> "engaged in arming and feeding..guerrilla bands in the vicinity."

Lt. Bird dismounted his men as skirmishers, and arrested Gregory.

On the return, a distance of nearly a mile, his command was fired upon from the woods. One man was killed, and two were severely wounded. Two horses were also hit, one of them being Lt. Bird's.

At the height of this exchange, Silas Gregory escaped into the swamp. As a result of this ambuscade, every farmer in the area was ordered to clear all underbrush skirting the roads, under the penalty of his property being destroyed for ignoring the order.[1]

Four days later, on October 17th, Colonel William Lewis' troops again encountered about 15 guerrillas. It was in a swampy, wooded area, some four miles from Camden Court House, and eight miles from South Mills. Federal carbineers were unsuccessful in engaging the hidden enemy, though Colonel Lewis lost 2 men killed and 1 wounded in the skirmish.[2]

As October and November passed, all Union activity increased by orders of Command at Fortress Monroe. Federal units scoured the countryside in search of horses, carts, fuel, forage, and contrabands. The primary objective of their search was the State Partisan Rangers, whom they called guerrillas. General Wild wrote of his concerns, on December 12th, to Brig. General Barnes, the Commander in Norfolk. Wild made frequent use of Federal gunboats, to reenforce his presence. He did remark, however, of his deep concern, whether the Confederates would send regular forces from Richmond.[3]

By mid-December, it had become evident to Captain W. Sanderlin, that the luck of his company was to shortly run out. The Federals were becoming increasingly outraged for their inability to exterminate the guerrillas. With each foray against the Federals, followed by his subsequent retirement to the swamp, Sanderlin knew their exact location would too soon become known. Discovery of the fallen-

Notes:
1. OR, Ser. I, Vol. XXIX, Pt. I, pgs. 481-482
2. OR, Ser. I, Vol. XXIX, Pt. I, pg. 484
3. OR, Ser. I, Vol. XXIX, Pt. II, pg. 562

log paths between infrequent spots of higher ground, combined with the desire to wipe them out, finally caused General Wild to issue orders for his men to search the swamp. This was by no means easy duty, as the water was from ankle to hip deep.

Cooler weather, however, had forced snakes into their dens, and leaves were down, tending to make the search somewhat easier. It's not hard to imagine pickets, guarding their camp-site, being disturbed by the splashing and clatter of the approaching searchers. Within minutes, the company members had gathered together their essentials, and had blended silently into the swamp on the opposite side of their island camp-site. As the Federals slogged onto higher ground, they discovered an organized camp. Cooking ovens had been made from bricks, carried into the swamp on the backs of men. There were small huts made of logs and mud. They were shelters for the men, and store houses. A few camp fires may have been burning with the usual assortment of pots and pans scattered about. Items of any size became victims of fire from the rifles of frustrated Federals.[1]

This general withdrawal by Sanderlin's men took place, around December 22, 1863. The date seemingly is accurate, according to subsequent reports of General Wild.

The General penned a brief message to General Barnes in Norkolk, on December 21, in which he enumerated his several expeditions to neutralize the partisan forces:

> "Three columns..traversed..Camden and..Currituck counties,..one landing at Powell's Point, marching north, another ferried across at Camden Court House,..marched down through Shiloh,..then up to Indiantown,..and the..third from..South Mills to Indiantown, then to Currituck Court House." 2

Edwd. A. Wild
Brig. Gen. Vols.

Notes:
1.OR, Ser. I, Vol. XXIX, Pt. I, pg. 913
  (Articles recovered in the mid-1970's had single bullet holes)
2.OR, Ser. I, Vol. XXIX, Pt. I, pgs. 910,911

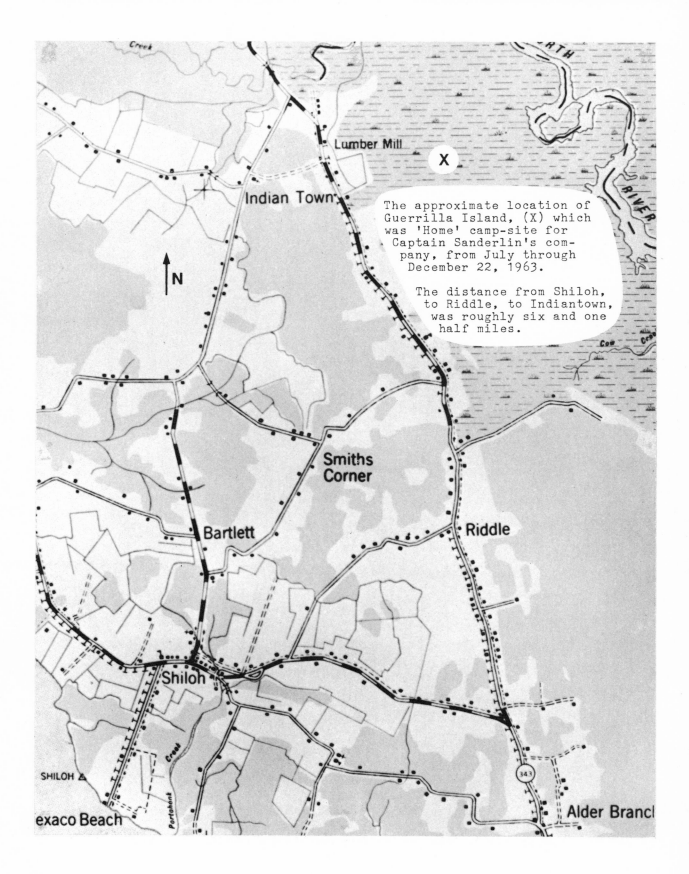

X

The approximate location of Guerrilla Island, (X) which was 'Home' camp-site for Captain Sanderlin's company, from July through December 22, 1963.

The distance from Shiloh, to Riddle, to Indiantown, was roughly six and one half miles.

In early March, 1985, the writer experienced the thrill of visiting grandfather William's first camp-site, after he had enlisted in Captain Willis B. Sanderlin's company, on June 6, 1863. It was on this elevated area in the swamp, near Indiantown, Camden County, (in time to be known as Guerrilla Island), that the company found shelter, while they harassed the Federal troops of General Wild. Discovered by William W. Forehand and Alex Leary, historians of Camden County, the island appears much as it did in 1863. Indeed, it has yielded a number of historical artifacts.

A shallow sub-surface probe revealed bricks which were carried in by hand, for use in small cooking ovens by the troops. Elliott, left, and Forehand, grandsons of Confederate Veterans, who inhabited the island, located the bricks.

Great activity persisted in the shipment of contrabands, by gunboat and schooner, to Roanoke Island. All other material was being readied for shipment to Norfolk. Wild continued, that he:

> "had some encounters with guerrillas..which resulted in the loss of..4 men killed,..7 wounded and 1 taken prisoner. Two more guerrilla camps, located deep..in the impenetrable swamps,..were burned,..also houses, barns,...and distilleries used by..the guerrillas. We also took..some of their relatives hostage, to be used in trade for our troops being held by the rebels. In the last two camps destroyed,..the men salvaged 40 to 50 good Enfield's and 1 drum"... 1

Had General Wild only identified which expedition had overrun Captain Sanderlin's island camp-site, it would be most useful for accurately reconstructing events leading to Sanderlin's withdrawal.

Seven days later, on December 28, 1863, after his return to Norfolk, General Wild submitted a very lengthy, and detailed, report to George H. Johnston, AAG, which elaborated upon his former dispatch to General Barnes, on December 21st. General Wild commented that he:

> "sent 250 men to land at Powell's Point, ferried 400 across to..Camden Court House,..all of whom marched to Indiantown,..where they met..Colonel Draper who had come north from Shiloh. Colonel Draper encountered..the guerrillas three times. At Shiloh..they had made a strong night attack, driving in his pickets,..and..pouring in volley after volley upon his camp-fires, with no effect. Colonel Draper..had withdrawn his men..to sleep inside the church,..leaving the..fires burning. The picket reserve, having been secretly posted, returned the fire, driving away the enemy before the Colonel could form..his men for pursuit. Next day he was waylaid again..at Sandy Hook by an estimated force of 200, who had taken a position at the swamp's edge, some 400 yards distant. They held their position..until the Colonel had brought up 300 men,..with two..flanking parties moving to..the right..and left. When a bayonet charge developed..from one flanking unit,...the

Note:
1.OR, Ser. I, Vol. XXIX, Pt. I, pgs. 910, 911

partisans disappeared in the swamp." 1

In this skirmish, 13 partisans and 11 Federals were killed. The continuation of General Wild's report describes what must have been the discovery, and destruction, of Captain Sanderlin's island campsite:

> "After crossing Indiantown Bridge the Colonel's rear guard was attacked again but the enemy was repulsed."

This encounter evidently occurred later in the day, after which the Colonel's troops made camp near the creek. The next day, December 22nd, General Wild's combined force:

> "returned to the swamp and after much searching and delay,..found their trail,..a succession of single..felled tree trunks, leading into..their citadel. We filed in single, burned their camp, took many guns, chiefly new Enfields(Tower Mark, 1863),considerable fine ammunition,drum,clothes, provisions, etc. After burning numerous cabins and huts and giving them another chase"... 2

the Federals marched to Currituck Court House, where they boarded their steamer, the Flora Temple. After daylight, on the 23rd, while preparing for departure of the entire contingent, General Wild was warned by Major White, of the cavalry, that rebels were approaching in force, with cavalry and artillery. He would be cut off.

As his strength was now reduced to 400 infantry, suffering fatigue, plus being encumbered by 73 teams and wagons, many contraband families, plus 2500 negroes, he felt it wise to withdraw. By boat and train, General Wild evacuated his position, retiring to both Roanoke Island and Norfolk. [3] In concluding his long report, General Wild was critical of North Carolina Governor Vance, in the man-

Notes:
1.OR, Ser. I, Vol. XXIX, Pt. I, pgs. 911-918
2.OR, Ser. I, Vol. XXIX, Pt. I, pgs. 911-918
3.OR, Ser. I, Vol. XXIX, Pt. I, pg. 913

ner he had organized the partisan forces. Wild also named some of the:

> "guerrilla..company..Captains,..among them were Sanderlin, Elliott, Etheridge, Hughes, Walston, and Grandy. All of their camps were located and destroyed." 1

Inclosure 'A' of his report constituted a timely warning to the citizens, that the Union would prevail:

> "General Butler intends to exterminate all guerrillas east of..Chowan River,..and will use any and all means..to do so. If it cannot..be..done otherwise,..property..of all sorts..will be destroyed,..and the country..entirely laid waste. If citizens wish to prevent..such universal destruction of their property,..they must aid our authorities..in ridding..this country..of these land pirates. It now..rests with them..to save themselves and property, or not. We have force now here sufficient..to accomplish our purpose, and shall immediately enter upon the work. Now is the time for the people to come forward."

Inclosure 'B' was addressed to:

> "the inhabitants of Currituck, Pasquotank, Perquimans, Gates, and Chowan counties."...

The General well emphasized the Union resolve, with warning for residents to:

> "give information against them (the guerrillas) to the military....by assisting them (the guerrillas) on their way with food and..transportation, you can save yourselves..the necessity of visitations from the colored troops."

Inclosure 'C' consisted of a list of Union citizens in Elizabeth City, on the road from Nixonton to Woodville, up Little River, Nixonton, on the road from Elizabeth City to Nixonton(Body Road), on the road from Elizabeth City, to the river bridge, and on the river road, and lower part of Pasquotank County. Wasn't he in error for Note:

1.OR, Ser. I, Vol. XXIX, Pt. I, pg. 916

not listing Camden County, in Inclosure 'B'?   1

Secretary of War, Edwin M. Stanton, received a final report from Major General Benjamin F. Butler, Headquarters, 18th Army Corps, Dept. of Virginia and North Carolina, dated December 31, 1863. In it Butler briefly summarized the six-month expedition of General Wild. He praised him for his most stringent measures.   An inclosure was the..'Petition of 523 Citizens of Pasquotank:'

> "At..a meeting..of the..citizens of..Pasquotank County, North Carolina, held at the Court House in Elizabeth City, December 19, 1863, Dr. William G. Pool being called to the chair and Isaiah Fearing selected secretary, a committee consisting of George W. Brooks, John C. Ehringhaus, R. F. Overman,..William H. Clark and..(by motion), William G. Pool were appointed to present suitable matter for the action of this meeting.
> Being called upon, George W. Brooks, Chairman, submitted the following preamble and resolutions which were unanimously adopted."

RESOLUTION

> "Whereas,..the County of Pasquotank has suffered immensely since the fall of Roanoke Island, without aid or protection from any source, and,
> Whereas, we have been lately visited, by order of General Benjamin F. Butler, by such force and under such..circumstance..as to cause universal panic and distress, and,
> Whereas, we have been assured by General E. A. Wild, in command of the force, that he will continue to operate here, even to the destruction, if necessary, of every species..of property for the purpose of 'ridding this country of partisan rangers,' and,
> Whereas, we believe that these..rangers cannot be of any service to us, but that their further presence here will bring upon us speedy and inevitable ruin, and,

Note:
1. OR, Ser. I, Vol. XXIX, Pt. I, pgs. 917,918

   Whereas,..we are promised to be 'let alone' if
these rangers..be moved or disbanded and return
quietly home, and further, if that..species..of
business known as 'blockade running'..be desis-
ted from, therefore, in view of these facts and
of this condition of things,
  Resolved: That we earnestly petition the Governor and Legislature of North Carolina, satis-
fied that you..cannot protect us with any force
at your command, to remove or disband these few
rangers, on motion,
  Resolved: That we denounce that species of business..carried on here by..private citizens for
private..gain..known as..'blockade running' and
that we..hereafter use our best efforts to suppress such trade."

Motions were passed to obtain signatures of every male citizen
of the county, to bear these proceedings to the Governor and Legislature, to meet with General Butler and determine if these proceedings would be satisfactory with him, to raise funds to defray
costs of these proceedings and to distribute results of such proceedings to counties of Chowan, Gates, Perquimans, Camden and Currituck. Adjournment followed with the committee signing all documents.[1]

General Butler concluded, with his command organization, which
listed the African Brigade, commanded by Brig. General Edward A. Wild,
reporting to Brig. General James Barnes, Headquarters at Norfolk and
Portsmouth, Virginia. The African Brigade was composed of the 55th
Massachusetts; 1st, 2nd, 3rd, North Carolina colored; and the 1st,
5th, and 10th U.S. colored troops.[2]

Notes:

1.OR, Ser. I, Vol. XXIX, Pt. II, pgs. 595-598
2.OR, Ser. I, Vol. XXIX, Pt. II, pg. 619

Thus it was that all citizens, of these counties, were forcibly denied the token protection against the Federal forces. An alternative was to suffer the depredations of General Wild's war of reprisal against civilians. Wild was furious. His vigorous pursuit of the valiant Home Guards, was exacerbated when his superior forces appeared unable to overcome the valiant resistance of Sanderlin's company.

Though they were called pirates, guerrillas, bandits, partisan rangers, or State Guards, it mattered not. It didn't affect their intention to repel the invaders.

Knowing of the impressive Federal strength and resolve, evident during the first six months of Captain Sanderlin's Camden company, one can envision the desperate circumstances of those 51 men.

They were 51 men against over 500, well-equipped, Federal troops. The Union commanders were greatly frustrated by their inability to suppress the Home Guards.

The 51 men felt a moral obligation to resist the invaders. Their strength came from youth, tenacity, spirit of survival, knowledge of the land, and family support. When combined, these factors were responsible for their creating such a furor in the Federal command.

By the time Wild's troops overran the island camp-site, deep in the woods near Indiantown, the company had disappeared in the green gloom, leaving behind, in their haste, the roster of Captain Sanderlin's company.

A Camden County resident published a biographical history of the County over thirty years ago. The author, Jesse Forbes Pugh, included the worthy mention of Captain Sanderlin's island camp-site. His narrative hinted of the loss of Sanderlin's company roster.[1]

In early 1979, Camden historian, William W. Forehand, received a letter from Frank F. Bushnell, of St. Petersburg, Florida. In a

Note:
1. Three Hundred Years Along the Pasquotank, by Jesse F. Pugh, pg. 182

round-about manner, the letter had been addressed to the Mayor of Camden. As there was no Mayor, and the letter being of historical interest, it was given to 'Billy' Forehand. Bushnell had realized, after reading Pugh's book, that a historical document he owned was the missing roster.

Billy Forehand telephoned me, as I lived in Florida not far from Frank Bushnell. After hearing Billy's story, I offered to meet Frank and examine the roster. That meeting was the beginning of our long friendship.

Frank allowed me to have the roster photocopied. Billy's copy was the first to be mailed. In the interim, Billy Forehand organized a camp-site search party. In the group that disappeared in the swampy woods, were Billy Forehand, Alex Leary, W. J. Wilson, Mr. and Mrs. James Whitehurst, Randy Pugh, Paul Kight, and a photographer-reporter from the Daily Advance newspaper in Elizabeth City. Their goal was to walk upon that 1863 hidden island camp-site, in the North River swamp. Their effort was rewarded, by finding that island.[1]

Over the years, from 1979 to 1987, I repeatedly tried to encourage Frank to sell me the roster. He knew how I aspired to own it, for grandfather's name was one of the 51 signers.

Finally, in early 1987, Frank agreed to swap the muster roll for an 1870 Springfield carbine in firing condition. I was able to acquire one rather quickly. His comment at the exchange moment was, "I guess we have dickered long enough."

After receiving the attentions of a museum art conservator, the muster is now framed and hangs on my wall.

The evacuation of their island camp-site, in late December, 1863, was the final event that forced the company to leave Camden County.

Note:
1. Daily Advance newspaper, Elizabeth City, N.C., pg.22, May 20, 1979

By a circuitous route, the company marched west to Jackson, in Northampton County, where they joined the 68th Regiment. Training activities were brief, before they moved on to Murfreesboro, North Carolina, and then to Weldon, early in 1864. Elements of the 68th were involved in raids on South Mills, under command of General M. W. Ransom. [1]

Colonel James W. Hinton, of Pasquotank County, was Regimental Commander. He had been promoted from the rank of Lt. Colonel, in the Eighth Regiment. [2]

Major E. C. Yellowley, had been promoted to that rank, in August, 1863. In October, 1863, he was again promoted to a Lt. Colonel of the 68th Regiment. [3]

Initially, the 68th was formed with companies from Princess Ann County, Virginia, and from the North Carolina counties of Currituck, Camden, Pasquotank, Chowan, Gates, Hertford, and Bertie. [4]

Authority to organize the Home Guards was extended to Brig. General Richard C. Gatlin, who also served as Adjutant General, State Services. The 68th Regiment would be raised, from men living, within the territory occupied by the Federal forces.

General Gatlin's responsibilities included the 67th and 68th Regiments, Infantry; the 1st Heavy Artillery Battalion; the 15th Cavalry Battalion (Wynn's); and the 14th Cavalry Battalion that later became the 79th Regiment. [5]

The 67th and 68th were mostly in eastern North Carolina. At different times they were joined with detachments from other commands, all under General Collett Leventhrope, and General Lawrence S. Baker. [6]

Notes:

1. N.C.Regiments, 1861-1865, by Walter Clark, Vol. IV, pg. 365
2. N.C.Regiments, 1861-1865, by Walter Clark, Vol. III, pg. 713
3. N.C.Regiments, 1861-1865, by Walter Clark, Vol. V, pg. 55
4. N.C.Regiments, 1861-1865, by Walter Clark, Vol. III, pg. 717
5. N.C.Regiments, 1861-1865, by Walter Clark, Vol. V, pg. 6
6. N.C.Regiments, 1861-1865, by Walter Clark, Vol. IV, pg. 440

Records of the 68th Regiment have been found very scant. There are, however, the personal recollections of John W. Evans, a former 4th Corporal of Company D. His reminiscence of the 68th, dated May 30, 1901, was written at his home in Manteo, North Carolina. In his later years, Evans had been a Clerk of the Superior Court, of Dare County. When the Roster (Moore's) was filed with the County Clerk, he became extremely concerned that so little information of the 68th Regiment was included. He was thus prompted to record his memories for Walter Clark's North Carolina Regimental Histories.

John Evans identified each company in detail. To simplify things, only the commanding officers are noted below. Each company of the 68th Regiment, at it's formation in July, 1863, is enumerated as:

"Company A-From Pasquotank. Captains John T. Elliott
              and Thomas H. Tamplin

Company B-From Camden. Captains Willis B. Sanderlin
              and F. M. Halstead

Company C-From Camden. Captain Caleb B. Walston

Company D-From Hertford. Captains Hillary Taylor
              and Levi Askew

Company E-From Hertford. Captain Langley Tayloe

Company F-From Bertie. Captains John T. Mebane
              and William M. Sutton

Company G.-From Pasquotank. Captain Cyrus W. Grandy

Company H-From Chowan. Captain Richard Keogh

Company I-From Gates. Captains R. H. L. Bond
              and W. M. Daughtry

Company K-From Hertford. Captain Simon B. Poole" 1

Note:
1.N.C.Regiments, 1861-1865,by Walter Clark, Vol. III, pg. 713

1864

On January 15, 1864, Colonel James W. Hinton, Commanding North
Carolina State Forces, with his Headquarters at Murfreesboro, North
Carolina, addressed a responding letter to Maj. General Benjamin F.
Butler, Commanding at Fort Monroe.

Colonel Hinton included a letter copy addressed by Brig. General
Wild to Captain John T. Elliott of the Sixty-Sixth Regiment, North
Carolina State Troops. He wrote:

> "From the general tenor of the letter (Wilds'),
> and from the fact that it is addressed to an offi-
> cer of my command, I am induced to believe that
> General Wild intended his threat against 'guer-
> rillas' to be applied to the officers and men of
> my command."

Continuing his response to Butler, Colonel Hinton informed him
that the 68th Regiment was organized under legal authority of the
Governor of the State, with regularly commissioned officers. Then
he asked if General Wild intended to consider any future prisoners
from the 68th Regiment as guerrillas, or would they be recognized
and treated as other prisoners of war?"

> "I have captured a goodly number of the officers
> and men of the U.S. Army and Navy and have uni-
> formly treated them as prisoners of war."

Colonel Hinton then called his (Butler's) attention to the fact
that the ladies mentioned in General Wild's letter were still held
in close confinement in Norfolk, and:

> "I want to know...whether it is your purpose to
> hold these ladies..as 'hostages'..for a soldier
> legitimately captured?"

He closed his letter with a request for a speedy reply. The Colonel's letter was a followup inquiry relating to the January 12,
1864, hanging of Federal Private Samuel Jordan, for which General
Wild took as hostages, Mrs. Munden and Mrs. Weeks.[1]

Note:
1.OR, Ser. II, Vol. VI, pg. 847

Although the 68th had been ordered into training after arrival at Jackson, in January, 1864, there is evidence that command segments were involved in the Confederate drive to overturn the Federal occupation of New Bern and Newport. In a report to Major R. S. Davis, AAG, New Bern, on February 7, 1864, Brig. General I. N. Palmer, Union Commander, noted that:

> "the following regiments..are represented among the deserters and prisoners,..the great mass of them being deserters, who appear to be too well satisfied to get in here: (the various commands represented as being held by the Federals were) North Carolina Regiments: First, Fourth, Eighth, Nineteenth, Twenty-First, Twenty-Fifth,..Forty-Fourth, Forty-Ninth, Fifty-First, Fifty-Fourth, Fifty-Ninth, Sixty-First, and Sixty-Eighth. General Martin..was known to have..4000 men for his assault on Newport." 1

An original 68th Regiment Co. B Field Roster notes the promotion of 3rd Sgt. William H. Elliott, effective April 30, 1864. His rank became that of 1st Sgt. Another entry covered the months from July 7, 1863, to April 30, 1864. It certified the pay period as 9 months and 24 days. 1st Sgt. William H. Elliott received $166.09.

On or about May 1, 1864, the regiment moved to Weldon, but remained there only a short time. On June 1st, the regiment reported 548 men present. Another muster, dated from May 1 to June 30, 1864, shows 1st Sgt. William H. Elliott was absent, and sick, in Camden County.

Captain Sanderlin certified the latter muster as complete, having signed as Company Commander. The final endorsement by Lt. Colonel E. C. Yellowley, noted under remarks:

> "Discipline: Bad,..Instruction: Good,..Military Appearance: Very Good,..Arms: Enfield Rifles,..Accoutrements: Complete,..Clothing: Good" 2

Notes:
1. OR, Ser. I, Vol. XXXIII, pg. 56
2. N.C. Archives, C. W. Collection, Box 63

Further observations of John W. Evans, note that:

> "on or about 1 May, 1864, the regiment moved to Weldon, and only remained a short time."...1

General Bragg, in Richmond, received a letter from Robert Strange, dated June 4, 1864. Mr. Strange was responding to Special Orders he had received from the Adjutant and Inspector General's office. The duties of Robert Strange were to survey the important bridges and the guards on the railroad line between Richmond, Virginia, and Wilmington, North Carolina. His survey included the Weldon Bridge among the fifteen strategic bridges (over the Roanoke River:)

> "Weldon Bridge-The importance of this bridge is well(known), defenses very extensive. Troops stationed in and around Weldon on the 1st instant were:

	Men
Sixty-Eighth North Carolina Regiment, Col. J. W. Hinton	548
Mallett's Battalion, Major Hahr	349
First Battalion Reserves, Major Broadfoot	269
Captain Shaw's Artillery company	29
Captain Cherry's Cavalry company, Fourth Regiment	63
Captain Chappell's Infantry company	32
Total	1,290

> The bridge guard consisted of thirty men, well-armed from the Sixty-Eighth North Carolina Regiment,..two commissioned officers, Colonel J. W. Hinton, commanding post." 2

Weldon, North Carolina, is almost due south of Richmond, Virginia, and about ten miles south of the North Carolina-Virginia State line. Municipal development has occurred generally south and west of the Roanoke River, obliterating the Confederate defense lines.

The overleaf Weldon area defense map, was completed on March 12, 1863, fifteen months before Robert Strange began his survey. 3

Notes:

1. N.C.Regiments, 1861-1865, by Walter Clark, Vol. III, pg. 717
2. OR, Ser. I, Vol. LI, Pt. II, pgs. 987,988
3. Weldon Memorial Library, Weldon, N. C.

Irregular, perimeter defense lines, northeast and south of the river, reveal how thoroughly the Confederate troops were deployed.

Just south of the river was the junction of two railroad lines. Protection of this iron lifeline was vital to the Confederacy, thus the heavy concentration of troops.

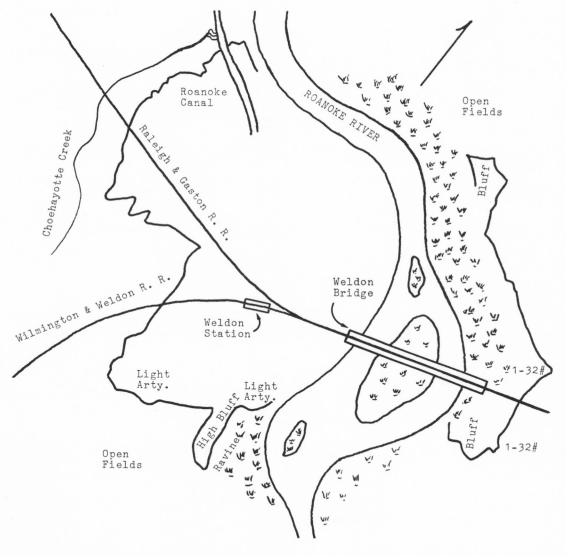

From the Federal records, there is what appears to be an intelligence report from John C. Babcock, to Major General A. A. Humphreys. General Humphreys was Chief of Staff at Headquarters, Army of the Potomac, Office of the Provost Marshall-General. The report, dated July 9, 1864, covering a multitude of events and personages, began:

"General: A deserter from the Twenty-Fifth North
Carolina Infantry, of Ransom's Brigade, Bushrod
Johnson's Division, that left..the hospital..at
Raleigh, N. C., on the 6th of June, 1864, and has
been at Weldon, N. C., until yesterday morning,..
gives the following information, which we think
reliable. At Weldon, Colonel Hinton's Regiment,
the Sixty-Eighth North Carolina, stationed on..
the south side of the Roanoke and a small force
of infantry and cavalry about two miles this side,
on the railroad, not more than 2000 in all. The
Sixty-Eighth North Carolina is the last regiment
in North Carolina, and is composed of conscripts,
many of whom are old soldiers. Informant remained
at Weldon from, the 6th of June till the 8th of
July." 1

An organization of troops, in the Department of North Carolina
and southern Virginia, commanded by General P. G. T. Beauregard, C.
S. Army, dated June 10, 1864, lists:

"The 68th North Carolina State Troops, infantry,
within command of the Second Military District,
(not reported)..." 2

Major William H. Bagley, of the 68th Regiment, resigned on the
11th of June, 1864. Colonel James W. Hinton promoted Captain Willis
B. Sanderlin to Major, effective the same day. Major Sanderlin retained command of Company B. 3

John W. Evans, then in his 56th year, continued to recall events
of the past. During the month of July, 1864, the regiment was sent
to Morganton, North Carolina, in the western part of the State.

A band of bushwhackers, known as Kirk's army, had, on June 28,
raided an encampment of Junior Reserves near Morganton:

"the then terminus of the Western North Carolina
railroad.".....

capturing more than one hundred of the Juniors late at night.

Notes:

1.OR, Ser. I, Vol. XL, Pt. III, pg. 97
2.OR, Ser. I, Vol. XXXVI, Pt. III, pgs. 891,892
3.N. C. Troops, by John W. Moore, Vol. IV, pg. 147

Marching orders for the 68th were received, and they proceeded under the command of Lt. Colonel E. C. Yellowley:

> "..along the graded railroad bed of the Western
> North Carolina railroad....then turned off..and
> crossed the Blue Ridge mountains at Bakersville,
> the county seat of Mitchell County, and on into
> Tennessee, known as the Crab Apple section"...1

No evidence of Kirk's army was found, so the regiment returned by the same route. It was thought the show of force would convince the marauders not to try further depredations against the populace.

Colonel G. W. Kirk commanded a band of renegade troops, about 400 cavalry and 200 infantry, who, though Southern, with a touch of Unionism, were greatly against the conscription of soldiers. Their objections took the form of raids on civilians and troops alike. [2]

It's possible 1st Sgt. William H. Elliott had returned for duty by July 31. The June 30th muster reported him sick in Camden County. [3]

There remains, to the best of my knowledge, a single, original Quartermaster document relating to the 68th Regiment, with a title of:

> "Account of clothing issued to enlisted men, Co.
> B, 68th N.C.S. Troops in the Q Muster ending....
> 30 September, 1864.
>
> Form No.   S3 July, August, September   1864
>
> We the..undersigned non commissioned..officers,
> artificers, musicians, privates, of Co. B, 68th
> Regiment N.C.S. Troops do hereby acknowledge to
> have received from..Captain Lewis O. Lawrence..
> A.A.Qm, the several articles of clothing set oppo-
> site our respective names"...

Grandfather William was issued only a jacket, pair pants, drawers, shirt, pair socks, pair shoes, cap, haversack, and overcoat. He was not issued a blanket, rucksack, or canteen. [4]

Notes:
1. N.C. Regiments, 1861-1865, by Walter Clark, Vol. III, pgs. 718, 719
2. N.C. Regiments, 1861-1865, by Walter Clark, Vol. III, pg. 758
3. N.C. Archives, C. W. Collection, Box 63
4. N.C. Archives, C. W. Collection, Box 63

Form No 33

We the Undersigned Non Commissioned Officers, Artificers, Musicians & privates of Co B 68th Regt N.C.S Troops do hereby acknowledge to have received from Capt Lewis C. Lawrence A.A.Q.M. the several Articles of Clothing Set opposite our respective names

Date of Issue 1864	Names of Soldier	Jackets	Pants Cotton	Drawers	Shirts	Shoes Cotton	Socks ( )	Blankets	Caps	H. Stocks	B. Stocks	Canteens	Overcoats		Signature	Witness
July Aug Sept	Enoch Sanderlin	0	1	0	1	1	1	0	0	0	0	1			Enoch Sanderlin	E.H. Stevens AA
	John Etheridge	0	1	0	1	1	1	0	0	0	0	1			John Etheridge	E.H. Stevens
	H. Earnheart	0	1	0	1	1	1	0	1	1	1	1			H. Earnheart	E.H. Stevens
	G. Earnheart	1	1	0	1	1	1	0	1	0	0	1			G. Earnheart	E.H. Stevens
	M. Woodhouse	0	1	0	1	1	0	0	0	1	0	1			M. Woodhouse	E.H. Stevens
	Peter Smith	0	1	1	1	1	0	0	1	0	0	1			P. Smith	E.H. Stevens
	J. Cox	0	1	0	1	1	0	0	0	0	0	0			Juley Cox X	E.H. Stevens
	John Wyatt	0	1	0	1	1	0	0	1	1	1	1			John Wyatt	E.H. Stevens
	George Cartright	0	1	0	1	1	0	0	1	1	0	1			George Cartright	E.H. Stevens
	J.S. Stephens	0	1	0	1	1	0	0	1	0	0	1			Joseph M. S. Stevens	E.H. Stevens
	Baily Dance	0	1	1	1	1	0	0	1	0	0	0			Baily Dance	E.H. Stevens
	N.C. Burgess	0	1	1	1	1	1	1	1	0	0	1			N. C. Burgess	E.H. Stevens
	Jas Abbott	0	1	0	1	1	0	0	1	0	1	1			Jas K. Abbott	E.H. Stevens
	M. Smith	0	1	0	1	1	1	0	1	1	1	1			M. Smith	E.H. Stevens
	John Foster	0	1	1	1	1	2	0	1	1	1	1			John Foster	E.H. Stevens
	Edgar Gilbert	0	1	0	1	1	0	0	1	1	1	1			Edgar B. Gilbert	E.H. Stevens
	W. Gregory	0	1	0	0	1	0	0	1	0	0	1			W. Gregory by T. Gregory	E.H. Stevens
	F.M. Holstead	0	1	0	0	1	0	1	1	0	0	0			F. M. Holstead	E.H. Stevens
	A. Gallop	0	1	1	1	1	0	0	1	1	0	1			A. Gallop	E.H. Stevens
	Saml Sivils	0	1	1	1	1	1	0	1	1	1	1			Saml Sivils	E.H. Stevens
	Caleb Everton	0	1	1	1	1	1	0	1	1	1	1				E.H. Stevens
	Edward Lamb	0	1	0	1	1	1	1	1	1	1	1				E.H. Stevens
	Levi Perkins	0	1	0	1	1	0	0	1	1	0	1			Levi Perkins	E.H. Stevens
	Major Gregory	0	1	0	1	1	0	0	1	0	0	1			Major T. Gregory	E.H. Stevens
	L.R. Wilson	1	1	0	1	1	0	0	1	0	0	1				E.H. Stevens
	Hilary Land	0	1	0	1	1	1	0	1	0	0	1				E.H. Stevens
	J. Sawyer	0	1	0	1	1	1	0	1	0	0	1				E.H. Stevens
	N.C. Sawyer	0	1	1	1	1	1	0	0	1	0	1				E. Williams
	W. Harris	0	1	0	1	1	1	0	0	1	0	1				E.H. Stevens
	C.J. Sawyer	0	1	1	1	1	1	0	0	1	0	1			C. Sawyer	E.H. Stevens
	W.J. Grandy	0	0	0	0	1	0	0	0	1	0	1				E.H. Stevens
	N. Sawyer	0	0	0	0	1	0	0	0	0	0	1			A. J. Sawyer	E.H. Stevens
	Charles Burfoot	1	1	0	1	1	1	0	0	0	0	1			Charles Burfoot	E.H. Stevens
⇨	William H. Elliott	1	1	1	1	1	0	0	1	0	0	1	⇨		William H. Elliott	E.H. Stevens
	Thomas Jones	0	1	0	1	1	0	0	0	0	0	1				E.H. Stevens
	Martin Etheridge	0	1	0	1	1	0	0	1	0	0	0			Martin Etheridge	E.H. Stevens
	James Gammons	0	0	1	0	1	1	0	0	0	0	1				E.H. Stevens
	Ro Roberts	0	0	0	1	1	1	0	0	1	0	1				E.H. Stevens
	John Tillit	0	1	0	0	1	0	0	0	0	0	1				E.H. Stevens
	Jesse Williams	0	1	0	1	1	0	0	0	0	0	1				E.H. Stevens
	R.M. Ellis	0	1	0	1	1	0	0	0	0	0	1			Robt M. Ellis	E.H. Stevens
	George Kick	1	1	0	1	1	0	0	0	0	0	1			George Kick	" " " "
	Charles Morriset	0	1	0	1	1	1	0	0	0	0	1				E.H. Stevens
	J. Mercer	1	1	0	1	1	0	0	1	0	0	1			Geo G. Mercer	E.H. Stevens
	Abel Gallop	1	1	0	1	1	0	0	1	0	0	1			Abel Gallop	E.H. Stevens
	Almon Morris	0	0	0	0	0	0	0	0	0	0	0				E.H. Stevens
	John C Fields	0	0	0	0	0	0	0	0	0	0	1			Jno C Fields	E.H. Stevens
	R.H. Davis	0	0	0	0	0	0	0	0	0	0	0			R H Davis	E.H. Stevens
	Total	6	45	17	37	46	37	00	15	55	3	15	45			

The men listed at random on Form S3, have been rearranged into alphabetical order for ease in reading.

James E. Abbott	F. M. Holstead
x Bailey Barco	x Thomas Jones
Charles Burfoot	George Kirk
N. C. Burgess	Edward Lamb
x George Cartright	x Hilory K. Land
Jubel Cox	John Mercer
R. N. Davis	x Almon Morris
G. Earnhart	Charles Morrisette
H. Earnhart	Levi Perkins
x William H. Elliott	R. Roberts
R. M. Ellis	Samuel Salyer
John Etheridge	Enoch Sanderlin
Martin Etheridge	x Samuel Savallo
x Caleb Everton	C. L. Sawyer
John E. Fields	x M. G. Sawyer
x John Foster	x N. Sawyer
Abel Gallop	x Peter Smith
x Kenneth Gallop	W. Smith
James Gammons	x Joseph W. Stevens
x Edgar B. Gilbert	x John Tillet
W. J. Grandy	Jesse Williams
x Major D. Gregory	John R. Wilson
Willoughby D. Gregory	M. Woodhouse
x William Harris	John Wyatt

Of this 48-man total, only 18 (marked with x), were signers of Captain Willis B. Sanderlin's roster at Shiloh, on June 6, 1863.

Within a few days after the Quartermaster issue on Sep 30, the 68th Regiment was ordered to supplement the guard force at Salisbury Prison, located roughly eighty miles east of Morganton, North Carolina.

The prison population consisted of Federal soldiers and deserters, as well as Confederate convicts. All were in almost constant conflict within the prison compound. In September, 1864, the office of commandant was vacated by the resignation of Colonel John A. Gilmer, due to failing health. Gilmer was replaced by the appointment of John H. Gee, of Quincy, Florida.

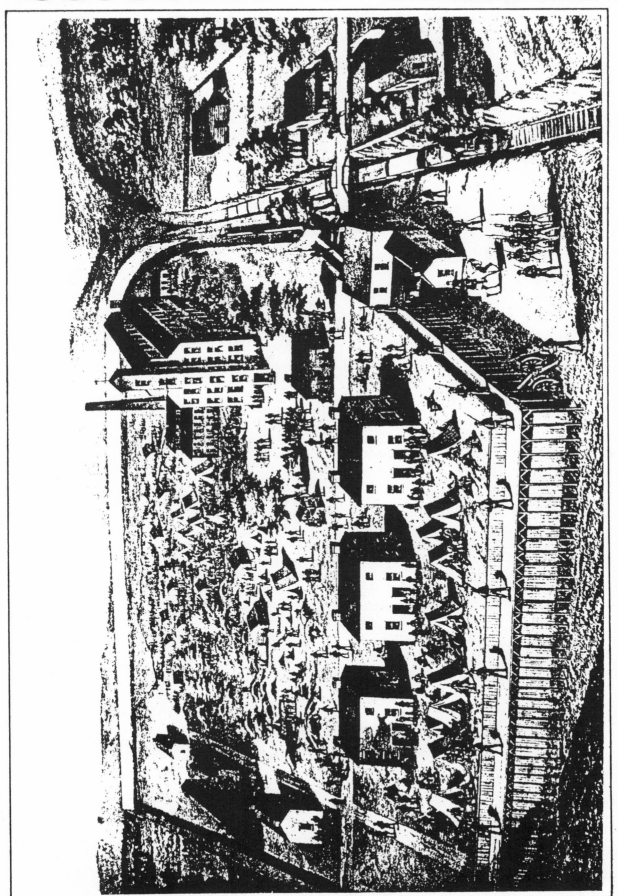

ARTIST'S IMPRESSION OF CONFEDERATE PRISON COMPOUND
SALISBURY, NORTH CAROLINA, 1864

Major Gee had been selected by General Bragg, as there were:

> "a number of hard cases at Salisbury, and Major
> Gee was appointed..to that place..on account of
> his prudence and discretion"....

A former Chaplain of the Sixth Regiment, North Carolina Troops, Rev. A. W. Mangum, provided an extremely detailed history of Salisbury Prison, from which both preceding, and following, observations have been borrowed:

> "By order of the War Department, General James G.
> Martin received about fifteen hundred guards, of
> whom over a thousand were Senior Reserves,.....
> and in 1864, the 68th Regiment served as prison
> guards. From October to the time they left there
> was no time(except perhaps while Colonel Hinton
> with the Sixty-Eighth Regiment was there),when,
> acting in concert and with determination,...the
> prisoners could not have overpowered..the guard
> and sacked..the town....On October 20,....about
> 2 o'clock in the afternoon, as the relief for the
> inside guard entered the prison, they were rush-
> ed upon and disarmed..by the prisoners, and two
> or three of them were killed....The citizens...
> (of Salisbury), apprehending..the cause..of the
> yells and firing, armed..themselves..as soon as
> possible and young and old came in haste to the
> prison.Colonel Hinton's Regiment (the 68th),which
> was on the train at the depot and about to leave,
> formed at the sound of the cannon,double quicked
> to the stockade and mounted the parapet,but these
> and the citizens came too late"....

The guards had prevailed, and effectively put down the riot, with 16 prisoners killed and 60 wounded. In all, the episode lasted about ten minutes. [1]

In October,...while the 68th was beginning guard duty at Salisbury Prison, General Robert E. Lee had begun a serious letter campaign to tap additional sources of troops.

Note:
1.N.C.Regiments, 1861-1865,by Walter Clark, Vol. IV, pgs. 745-768

On October 8th, General Lee's Headquarters was at Chaffin's Farm, south of Richmond. Lee's letter to General T. H. Holmes, Commanding North Carolina Reserves, at Raleigh, began with:

> "General: It is of the...utmost importance that this Army should be strengthened to enable it to cope with the greatly superior and daily increasing force of General Grant....the Sixty-Seventh North Carolina at Kinston be relieved by Junior Reserves. The Sixty-Eighth North Carolina is at Morganton, and should other troops..be required there, could not they be relieved..by reserves? The Sixty-Seventh and Sixty-Eighth Regiments are in the State service, but I will write to Governor Vance, who I believe takes as deep an interest in the..defense of the whole country.....to know if, there is any objection to turning them over to the Confederate service....if they cannot be assigned to duty with me till the campaign closes"....

Federal forces of Generals Grant, Butler, and Ord, were creating immense pressure on General Lee, during their campaign to capture Richmond. As this threat was considered by Lee to be most serious, he personally led the defense along the James River south of Richmond. The same day he wrote General Holmes, General Lee addressed a letter to Governor Z. B. Vance, of North Carolina. He stated why more troops were urgently needed in Virginia. Superior Federal numbers were extending their flanks in both directions, in an effort to envelope the Confederates. General Lee asked:

> "If there is any objection..to turning over the Sixty-Seventh and Sixty-Eighth Regiments to the Confederate Government, will circumstances permit your assigning them..to duty under me..till the active campaign ceases?" 1

Within a few days after General Lee had posted his letter to Governor Vance, the Governor responded, on October 25th, with an explanation why he was unable to release the 68th to the Confederate

Note:
1.OR, Ser. I, Vol. XLII, Pt. III, pgs. 1141,1142

Army in Virginia. On October 29, 1864, General Lee responded to the Governor's letter:

> "....and while I regret the facts you state,..I thank you for your efforts..on our behalf. I am gratified to hear what you say of the home guards and reserves and trust..that you will bring out as many as possible. With reference to the Sixty-Seventh and Sixty-Eighth Regiments, I understand that one is in western North Carolina(the 68th) ....I would therefore advise that whichever one of the regiments..above referred to..is in west North Carolina be sent..to Wilmington to aid in the defense of that place"... 1

Governor Vance must have approved transfer of the 68th to Wilmington after their duty at Salisbury. From his headquarters in Wilmington, North Carolina, Major General W. H. C. Whiting, on November 23, 1864, wrote General Hebert, commanding at Fort Fisher:

> "The movement is ordered...by the President and General Lee,...the former ordering General Bragg to use his judgement,...the latter directing him to take all available troops from Wilmington... I have ordered..the Sixty-Eighth North Carolina (Hinton's) to come down the railroad at once. Will use it to replace the detachments until they return. I am commanding the department till Bragg returns"... 2

Late in 1864, Companies A and F, Sixty-Fifth North Carolina Regiment, together with Lee's (Alabama) battery, and several companies of the Fiftieth Regiment, were stationed at Williamston, North Carolina. They were a deterrent against an expected Federal drive north, from either Washington or Plymouth. Williamston was 22 miles west of Plymouth, both on the south side of the Roanoke. West of Williamston were Spring Green Church, Butler's Bridge, the Sherrod House, Fort Branch, and Hamilton. These locations would become prominent in the forthcoming engagement. 3

Notes:

1.OR, Ser. I, Vol. XLII, Pt. III, pg. 1183
2.OR, Ser. I, Vol. XLII, Pt. III, pg. 1227
3.N.C.Regiments, 1861-1865,by Walter Clark, Vol. III, pgs.681-722

The chronicles of the Sixty-Fifth North Carolina Regiment were written by former Captain M. V. Moore, Regimental Assistant Quartermaster. Moore set his name to the record on April 26, 1897, in Auburn, Alabama. He described the action as it occurred:

> "....the enemy came up from below...and a sharp fight between two companies of cavalry with Lee's Battery and..the enemy, took place 11 December, (1864) at Spring Green...our small force, faced by over 1,000 of the enemy, fell back on the 12th to Butlers Bridge near Hamilton, where they were reenforced..of the Seventieth hurried back from Tarboro (with) the Sixty-Eighth..Though several hundred of the enemy, who, piloted by a traitor, crossed the stream below...and fired upon us in our rear during the night. They were driven back with small loss to us except the capture of Colonel Hinton and his Adjutant of the 68th"... 1

The 10th North Carolina Regiment was encamped near Fort Branch (about five miles east of Hamilton on the Roanoke River), and was awaiting the Federals, in December, 1864. A force of Federals consisting of infantry, cavalry, and artillery, were known to be advancing from Plymouth, reaching the vicinity of Fort Branch in the night of December 11th:

> "Colonel James W. Hinton with his regiment, the Sixty-Eighth North Carolina, was moving from... Tarboro to meet the enemy...before day Sergeant Pool was sent to communicate with Colonel Hinton and inform him of the situation. Riding into the midst of the enemy, mistaking them in the darkness for Colonel Hinton's command,...he was captured, and found Colonel Hinton also a prisoner. Colonel Hinton, with his Adjutant, Captain Joseph Hinton, riding in advance..of his regiment, met the Federal advance. Captain Hinton in the darkness succeeded in escaping and reached the regiment (68th) safely." 2

Once again it is John W. Evans who has provided extreme detail

Notes:

1.N.C.Regiments, 1861-1865, by Walter Clark, Vol. III, pgs.680,681
2.N.C.Regiments, 1861-1865, by Walter Clark, Vol. I, pg. 527

of the encounter, on December 12, 1864. The Federals advancing from the vicinity of Plymouth (to the east), planned to attack a fort at Rainbow Banks, near Hamilton. Their objective, was Fort Branch.

The 68th received their marching orders while in Tarboro:

> "We were ordered on a hasty march in the afternoon, of December 12, 1864, and marched with an occasional rest till dark"...

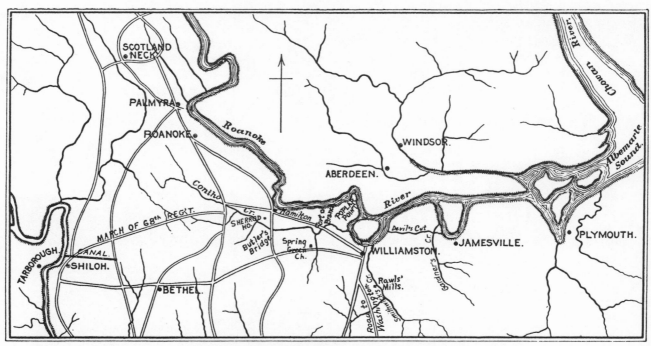

MAP OF BUTLER'S BRIDGE AND VICINITY.

In the midst of pine thickets, a camp was pitched. The weather was clear and cold, with temperatures falling. Each soldier made his own bed on pine straw, and slumbered fitfully during the cold darkness. At midnight they were awakened by the long drum roll, a signal to be in readiness quickly, followed by marching orders. In darkness they marched ten miles over frozen ground. At Butler's Bridge, two miles south of Hamilton, there were four companies of the Seventieth North Carolina, two companies from the Sixty-Fifth, and a section of Lee's Battery, stationed at the (Coniho) creek.

(continued page 60)

Camp Baker, just east of Hamilton, was established close to the Sherrod house. It was here the 70th North Carolina Regiment placed their headquarters. Visiting Confederate forces also camped in the general area while assigned to Fort Branch.

The Sherrod house was a part of former Camp Baker. Here Colonel James W. Hinton with his Adjutant and brother, Captain Joseph Hinton, sought lodging the night before the battle of Butler's Bridge. Minutes after mounting their horses before dawn the next morning, both were captured. (see narrative page 61)

It was down this road that the 68th marched before dawn, on the way to Butler's Bridge. As it happened, the Union and Confederates were silently marching side by side in the dark. When their identities became known, each side took cover at roadside as an ineffective skirmish ruptured the silent dawn.(see narrative page 60)

Butler's Bridge spanned swampy Coniho Creek. Marking the original crossing site on the south side, is a long-abandoned foundation. Horses galloping across the bridge from the Confederate side, just before daylight, were thought, by the Union, to be the Confederate cavalry. (see narrative page 60)

Spring Green Primitive Baptist Church was established in 1811. This original structure, still in use, was the destination of re- treating Union troops, after the battle of Butler's Bridge.

(see narrative page 61)

The interior of Fort Branch, looking eastward from the entrance, is clear of brush. A majority of the earthwork fortifications are clearly defined, as are a line of rifle pits extending southward.

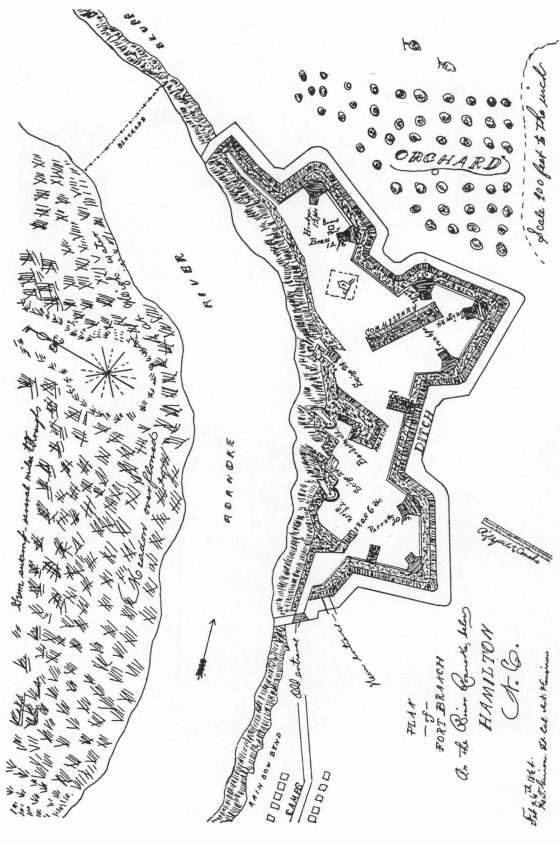

A sketch of Fort Branch, prepared by Lt. Colonel Henry T. Guion. Colonel Guion commanded Companies F, G, H, and K of the First North Carolina Artillery. The fort was named in honor of Brig. General Lawrence O. Branch, a native North Carolinian from nearby Enfield.

Fort Branch occupied a most strategic location at a bend in the Roanoke River.

High on a bluff, on the south bank, the fort commanded an unobstructed firing zone in both directions.

Remains of rifle pits extending southward of the earthworks are yet visible.

The fort, a historical site, is privately owned by Mr. Henry Winslow, a local planter.

Travelers are welcomed, but must be escorted.

There are, to the best of my knowledge, no contemporaneous images
depicting attempts by the Union Army to capture Fort Branch.

A 'living history' weekend, and reenactment at the fort, permitted the pictorial impressions on this, and the following page.

Above, is a section of the Confederate defenders encampment. An
early morning rifle drill, in the field outside the original rifle
pits, is below.

The Confederate skirmish line.

A Union cavalry party scouting perimeter of the fort.

> "The enemy, piloted by some buffaloes(traitors)
> crossed the creek below (the east) and took our
> troops at the bridge in the rear. We had turned
> off from the main road from Tarboro to Williams-
> ton in order to come in by Hamilton to reenforce
> from the rear our troops at Butlers Bridge."

The term buffaloes, commonly referred to renegade bands in eastern North Carolina, composed of armed negroes, native Union bushwhackers, and criminally-intentioned local misfits. They preyed on
the prosperous and poor alike, relying on brutality for their suc-
cess.

After the 68th passed through, or around, the village of Hamilton
before dawn, they marched south down the road to Butler's Bridge.
By coincidence, the Federals, who had arrived from the east, turned
left on the same road, and also marched south. Both the Union and
Confederate troops were wearing long cape overcoats, and so in the
darkness became intermingled:

> "Lt. Colonel Yellowley (the 68th acting command-
> er) and the Colonel or officer...commanding the
> Federal troops were riding side by side. Yellowley
> supposed the other horseman was Colonel Hinton's
> body servant, riding an extra horse for Colonel
> Hinton. He did not discover to the contrary until
> the Federal officer gave a command to the person
> riding by his side, supposing him to be his courier"

Colonel Yellowley, who hadn't responded to the command, was then
recognized by the Federal officer, as 'the enemy.' Simultaneously
both officers alerted their commands, who took cover at roadside.
A face-to-face skirmish developed. Each side captured some of their
own men, but few casualties resulted, because of darkness. When the
encounted ended, the Federals were between the 68th and the bridge,
causing Yellowley's command to fall back towards Hamilton:

> "....but the troops at..Butlers Bridge,...though
> flanked front and rear, escaped by the fact that
> the cavalry was dismounted for skirmishing,....
> their horses which were held in the rear (north)
> were stampeded by the sudden firing behind them,
> broke loose and charged across the bridge...the

enemy in front (south side of the river),..were
stampeded by this,..supposing we were advancing
in force and our forces...saved...themselves by
crossing over and turning to the right,..up the
road to Tarboro. The enemy had turned to the left
(east) going back towards Spring Green Church." 1

In those dark hours just before dawn, either elements of Federal
troops, or buffaloes acting in their support, passed just west of
the road, from Hamilton, to Butler's Bridge. They approached the Sherrod house, almost a mile northwest of the bridge. Colonel Hinton,
and his brother, Captain Joseph Hinton, the Regiment Adjutant, were
captured. Both men were completely surprised by the suddenness of
a skirmish in the dark. They had been at the Sherrod house most of
the night, and were on their way to join the regiment before dawn.

Not long after the break of day, Captain Hinton escaped. The Captain was indeed lucky, for he carried in his pocket a leave-of-ab-
sence to return home. He was to be married, and he didn't disappoint
his bride-to-be." 2

The Federals continued down the road from the bridge, to Spring
Green. They were then chased along the Williamston road, with the
Confederates close behind.

Colonel James W. Hinton spent the rest of the war in a Federal
prison. Lt. Colonel Yellowley was promoted to commander of the 68th
Regiment.

One might easily conclude that Major General W. H. C. Whiting, at
Wilmington, was becoming more irritated by his inability to obtain
reenforcements for area defense. In another letter on December 30,
1864, General Whiting reviewed his plight with Lt. Colonel A. Anderson. Anderson was the Assistant Adjutant, and Inspector General,
of the Department of North Carolina. In conclusion, he wrote:

Notes:
1.N.C.Regiments, 1861-1865,by Walter Clark, Vol. III, pgs.720-722
2.N.C.Regiments, 1861-1865,by Walter Clark, Vol. IV, pg. 17

> "I suggest an exchange for the reserves, that the
> remaining companies of the Tenth Regiment being
> artillery, be sent here, together with the 68th,
> for the purpose"... 1

A followup communication from Major General Whiting to A. A. G.
Lt. Colonel A. Anderson, on December 31, 1864, carried an increased tone of urgency:

> "Colonel. Please to ask the General (Bragg) if,
> until the arrival of troops for the city garri-
> son, he will authorize..General Hoke to furnish
> suitable details for guard duty....on my requi-
> sition,...the removal of the reserves, the dis-
> banding of the home guards, and the return of the
> department battalion,..to their work on details
> makes it absolutely necessary for me to press my
> request of yesterday for..the Tenth North Caro-
> lina and the Sixty-Eighth"...

General Whiting's letter was returned to him the same date from
Headquarters, Department of North Carolina, with the endorsement:

> "Respectfully returned. Hoke's Division is held
> for a special purpose, and it is not deemed ad-
> visable to use it..as indicated. It is supposed
> that all the duties proposed can be performed by
> the senior reserves, the artillery, and cavalry.
>
> By Order of General Bragg:
>
>   A. Anderson
>   Assistant Adjutant-General 2

Notes:
1. OR, Ser. I, Vol. XLII, Pt. III, pg. 1357
2. OR, Ser. I, Vol. XLII, Pt. III, pgs. 1359, 1360

1865

An abbreviated second history of the 68th Regiment was written by W. T. Caho, former 4th Sergeant, Company C. His narrative of the 68th Regiment's participation in the Wilmington campaign discloses that Company C was detailed as train guards on the Wilmington and Weldon railroad. They were also on river steamers on the Cape Fear River from Wilmington to Fayetteville, and had duties in and around Wilmington, in the fall of 1864. After the capture of Fort Fisher, and the evacuation of Wilmington, in January, 1865, his company joined the Regiment, then encamped on the Roanoke River near Fort Branch:

> "There we remained for a few days until the regiment was ordered to Williamston to gather commisary stores. From there the regiment was ordered to Tarboro, thence to Goldsboro, and Kinston,.. where, we met the advance of General Schofield's army at Wise's Forks. On their march from New Bern to Goldsboro...the regiment was engaged in that fight over the 8th and 9th of March. In falling back to Goldsboro...just before the Bentonville battle they (the 68th) engaged the extreme right wing of Sherman's army...at Cox's bridge on the Neuse River between Goldsboro and Smithfield."[1]

The January 31, 1865, organization of troops, in the Department of North Carolina, General Braxton Bragg, C. S. Army, Commanding, began with the Second Military District.

The Commander of the Second District was Brig. General Lawrence S. Baker. Reporting to General Baker was Col. Stephen D. Pool, Commanding the First Sub-District at Goldsboro.

Among those elements reporting to Colonel Pool was the 68th North Carolina, Lt. Colonel Edward C. Yellowley, Commanding. [2]

Ten days later, an organization of troops, Department of North Carolina, Major General Robert F. Hoke, C. S. Army, Commanding, dated February 10, 1865, noted that Brig. General Lawrence S. Baker, was assigned as Commander of the Second Military District.

Notes:
1. N.C.Regiments, 1861-1865, by Walter Clark, Vol. III, pgs. 709,727
2. OR, Ser. I, Vol. XLVI, Pt. II, pg. 1186

The Third Sub-District at Fort Branch was commanded by Colonel Frank S. Armistead. It included the 68th Regiment; 1st Junior Reserves; 6th North Carolina Cavalry; Co's A and F of Dicken's Battery; Lee's Battery (Alabama); and the 10th North Carolina Artillery. [1]

Thomas J. Brown, former Major of the Forty-Second North Carolina Regiment (Kirkland's Brigade), wrote his memoirs at home in Winston, North Carolina, on April 26, 1901. Of the events leading up to, and including, the battle of South West Creek (Wyse Fork), the 8th, 9th, and 10th of March, 1865, Brown wrote:

> "In a short time the Confederates reached Goldsboro (after leaving Wilmington),...the objective of three Federal armies. Sherman from the south, an army from Wilmington,...and an army from New Bern. It was seen that these armies must be fought separately...General Hoke's Division, supported by the Sixty-Seventh and Sixty-Eighth North Carolina, met the army from New Bern just below Kinston on the southeast shore of the Neuse (River) near Wise's Forks. It (the Federal Army) was commanded by General J. D. Cox."...

Confederate forces were deployed on the west bank of South West Creek, some three miles east of Kinston. Seasoned veterans of General's Robert F. Hoke's and D. H. Hill's Divisions awaited the Union forces when they arrived on the morning of March 8. [2]

The Confederate frontal assault on March 8th was fierce and effective. Between 1,500 and 1,800 Union prisoners were taken from the 15th Connecticut and 27th Massachusetts regiments. On March 9th both armies only skirmished.

Early in the morning on March 10 the Confederates, fully realizing they were greatly outnumbered, attempted an attack around the Union's left flank. [3]

Notes:
1. OR, Ser. I, Vol. XLVII, Pt. II, pg. 1155
2. N.C.Regiments, 1861-1865,by Walter Clark, Vol. IV, pg. 54
3. N.C.Regiments, 1861-1865,by Walter Clark, Vol. II, pgs.802,803

Finding the Union positions too strong, they returned to their lines. That night General Bragg evacuated Kinston, leaving behind Hoke's Division. As General Sherman had almost reached Averasboro, General Hoke's Division was sent to Bentonville, by way of Smithfield.

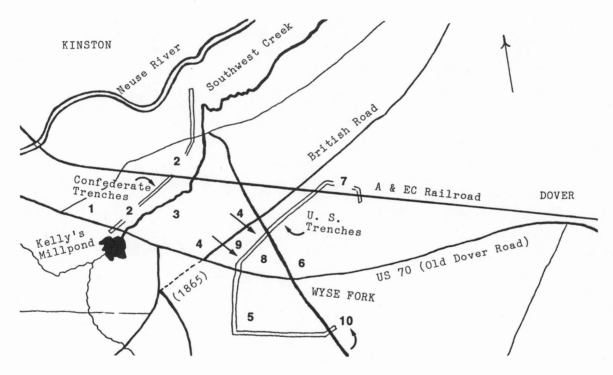

1. Confederate Headquarters
2. Confederate lines, Mar. 7-8
3. Capture of U. S. forces, (Upham's Brigade) by Hoke's Div.
4. Confederate lines, Mar. 8-10
5. U. S. line (Carter's Div.) Mar. 8-10
6. U. S. Headquarters
7. U. S. lines, Palmer's Div.
8. U. S. lines, Ruger's Div.
9. Confederate secondary attack, Mar. 10
10. Confederate main attack, Mar. 10

Reminiscences of the 17th Regiment were written by Wilson G. Lamb from his home in Williamston, N. C., on April 26, 1901. Lamb was a former 2nd Lieutenant of Company F. The closing days of the war in North Carolina saw the 17th Regiment at Goldsboro, the focal point of the three Federal armies:

> "Sherman with 70,000 men was advancing northward. Schofield, with his army corps of 26,000 raised the Federal forces to 30,000 at Wilmington, and Cox's Division...arriving at New Bern increased Palmer's command to 15,000.....The hope of successful resistance...was indeed forlorn and the only chance of any success was...to fight these armies separately. The column under General Cox advancing from New Bern....was encountered near Wise's Forks on the 8th of March (1865), by Hoke's Division....reenforced by the Sixty-Seventh and Sixty-Eighth North Carolina."...

The Sixty-Eighth also fought alongside the brigades of Kirkland, Hagood, and Colquitt, as well as the Sixty-Sixth Regiment commanded by Colonel Nethercut, a native of eastern North Carolina. [1]

Lt. Colonel Rufus W. Wharton, formerly of the Sixty-Seventh Regiment, completed his memoirs at Washington, D. C., in 1901. A portion of Wharton's narrative reveals that Federal General J. D. Cox led the advance from New Bern to Kinston. He was to join General Sherman, approaching from South Carolina. Wharton recalled that the 67th and 68th were participants in the battle of South West Creek, or Wyse Fork:

> "The two armies met at...South West Creek, four and a half miles east of Kinston, where for two days, 8th and 9th of March, 1865, there was sharp fighting, mostly by the Division of General R. F. Hoke, to which the Sixty-Seventh was attached.. After contesting the advance..of the enemy four days,..General Bragg withdrew to the north side of the Neuse (River), destroyed the bridge over the same and marched in the direction of Goldsboro. General Hoke...with his Division remained in the vicinity of Kinston two or three days longer and then joined Bragg at Goldsboro. At Goldsboro the Sixty-Seventh and Sixty-Eighth, the latter commanded by Lt. Colonel Edward C. Yellowley, were formed into a brigade and placed under command of Colonel John N. Whitford, of the Sixty-Seventh. At that time the Sixty-Seventh reported

Note:
1. N.C.Regiments, 1861-1865, by Walter Clark, Vol. II, pgs. 10,11

700 for duty and the Sixty-Eighth 300. The Sixty-Seventh and Sixty-Eighth were ordered from Goldsboro to a bridge over the Neuse River...a short distance east of Bentonville.....We reached the bridge about noon....when the enemy appeared in large numbers on the opposite...the south side. On that side the river is bordered...by a swamp about a half mile wide"...

A skirmish line was posted. The remainder of the brigade formed a line on the north side, to the left and right of the bridge. Just after daylight, the Federals attacked, driving back the skirmishers, who quickly recrossed the bridge, setting it on fire.

When the bridge was nearly consumed, the brigade withdrew. Their objective had been to prevent the enemy crossing during the battle of Bentonville. A day or two after the battle, the brigade joined General Joseph Johnston's army at Smithfield, where they remained one day, and then marched east, by way of Wilson and Tarboro. This was to have been a move toward the enemy's rear, to destroy transportation and supplies. Upon reaching Tarboro, the 68th remained, and the 67th moved on to Greenville. [1]

John W. Evans, in his recollections of the battle of South West Creek, observed that, a short time after the engagement at Butler's Bridge, the Sixty-Eighth was ordered to a position just below Kinston. They reenforced General Hoke at a place known as Cobb's Mill. There, a heavy battle known as the battle of South West Creek, or Wyse Fork, was fought on March 8 and 9, 1865:

"The Sixty-Eighth was moved after the battle to a bridge across the Neuse River, a short distance from Goldsboro, and remained there till the Federal forces had...advanced from Kinston and had stopped on the opposite side of the river...for a day and night. A light skirmish took place there. The bridge was then burned. Then we moved eastward, making no permanent stops. As we did this, orders were given....to the officers of several

Note:
1. N.C. Regiments, 1861-1865, by Walter Clark, Vol. III, pgs. 708, 709

companies to return with their men..to the com-
munities from which...they were mustered, seize
horses and return...for reenlistment as cavalry
service." 1

It cannot be determined if grandfather William was among the men
ordered to return home and obtain mounts.

Lt. Colonel A. Anderson, A. A. G., released an effective strength
report, on March 17, 1865. General Hoke's Division had a total of
4,775 men. Colonel Anderson concluded with a memorandum:

"In the report of troops of Department of North
Carolina, Col. Whitford, Commanding Sixty-Seventh
and Sixty-Eighth North Carolina Regiments belong
to Hoke's Division, but being at Goldsboro, their
strength is only approximated"... 2

Judging from this report, the 68th had only remained briefly at
Fort Branch before it was ordered to reenforce Hoke's Division at
Wyse Fork, on March 8th, 9th, and 10th. Then, they hurriedly return-
ed to the vicinity of Goldsboro.

An extract from the March 17th Field Return, of Hoke's Division,
notes that:

"Colonel Whitford's command of the Sixty-Seventh
and Sixty-Eighth North Carolina Regiments...now
belong to Hoke's Division...but being at Goldsboro, only an approximate estimate of the force
can be given..the Sixty-Seventh North Carolina,
about 700, Sixty-Eighth North Carolina Regiment
about 300, total 1,000"... 3

Notes:

1. N.C. Regiments, 1861-1865, by Walter Clark, Vol. III, pg. 722
2. OR, Ser. I, Vol. XLVII, Pt. II, pg. 1408
3. OR, Ser. I, Vol. XLVII, Pt. II, pg. 1424

Six days later, on March 23rd, a field return of troops in the Department of North Carolina, contained a memorandum:

> "Junior Reserves...the Sixty-Seventh and Sixty-Eighth North Carolina Regiments are marching to join General Hoke, and no report is yet received of them"...

> Respectfully submitted   Braxton Bragg
>   General   1

An effective strength report was again issued by Colonel Anderson. In covering the period of March 17th, 23rd, and 27th, he concluded with a memorandum:

> "Colonel Whitford's command, consisting of Sixty-Seventh and Sixty-Eighth North Carolina Regiments belong to Hoke's Division, but being at Goldsboro their strength is only approximated"...

The effective strength of infantry in Hoke's Division, on March 17th was 4,775 men. There were an additional 782 men assigned artillery. On March 23rd, his effective strength showed a reduction in infantry to 3,598 men, as well as an artillery reduction to 657 men. No reports from Hoke's Division were received for March 27th.[2]

A final abstract from the March 31, 1865 return for General Joseph E. Johnston concluded with another memorandum:

> "The Sixty-Eighth..and Sixty-Seventh..Regiments North Carolina State Troops, and the First North Carolina Battalion (State).....operating on the enemy's communications...with New Bern, are not reported" 3

The mid-March orders, to obtain horses, were being carried into effect, when word came of General Lee's surrender. Members of the several companies, absent while foraging for horses, are not known to have returned for discharge, and mustering out. [4]

Notes:
1. OR, Ser. I, Vol. XLVII, Pt. II, pg. 1462
2. OR, Ser. I, Vol. XLVII, Pt. III, pgs. 706,707
3. OR, Ser. I, Vol. XLVII, Pt. III, pg. 731
4. N.C. Regiments, 1861-1865, by Walter Clark, Vol. III, pgs. 722,727

In April, 1865, the career of the Sixty-Eighth Regiment, North Carolina Troops, came to an end. The regiment was mustered out of service near Wilson, North Carolina. There were no formalities of a surrended. Simply put, the 68th Regiment was discharged, and all men were told to go home. [1]

Over a period of some fifteen months, from late December, 1863, until the end of March, 1865, the Sixty-Eighth Regiment was, indeed, well-used to help defend eastern North Carolina. An original Regimental use-plan was developed by General Richard C. Gatlin.

I'm guessing that the Sixty-Eighth had moved by foot, although there were the welcome rides on those Western North Carolina, Wilmington and Weldon, Raleigh and Gaston, North Carolina, and Atlantic and North Carolina railroads.

The Sixty-Eighth acted as support troops, seeing major service at the following North Carolina areas: Murfreesboro, Weldon, Morganton, Bakersville, Salisbury Prison, near New Bern, Hamilton, Fort Branch, Butler's Bridge, Tarboro, Kinston, South West Creek, Goldsboro and Smithfield, as well as on the western slopes of the Bald Mountains in eastern Tennessee. (see map page 71)

There is little doubt that other skirmishes occurred, though no evidence of such encounters has yet been discovered.

For an unknown reason, at an unknown time and place, grandfather William was promoted from 1st Sergeant to Lieutenant, in late 1864.

Four documents are possessed by the author, which indicate his promotion did occur. Firstly, the Roster of the William F. Martin Camp 1590, United Confederate Veterans, in Elizabeth City, states that my grandfather William joined at the annual meeting, on August 11, 1910. [2] (continued page 72)

Notes:
1. N.C.Regiments, 1861-1865, by Walter Clark, Vol. III, pg. 727
2. Museum of the Albemarle, Elizabeth City, North Carolina

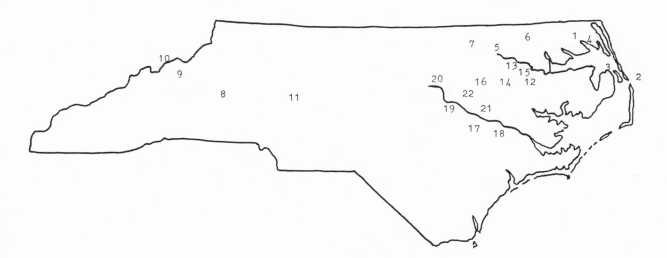

Identified above, are the major action areas listed below, during the military career of my grandfather, William H. Elliott. He first enlisted in Company L, of the 17th North Carolina Regiment, (First Organization). In his second enlistment, he was eventually assigned to Company B, of the 68th Regiment, North Carolina Troops. Grandfather's military service began, on May 4, 1861, and ended in April, 1865, when he was mustered out.

1. Elizabeth City.
2. 1st Enlistment, Oregon Inlet, 17th Regiment, Company L.
3. Roanoke Island surrender.
4. 2nd Enlistment, Camden County, Captain Sanderlin's company.
5. Jackson, basic training.
6. Murfreesboro, Reg't training.
7. Weldon.
8. Morganton.
9. Bakersville.
10. Tennessee area, pursuit of Kirk's army.
11. Salisbury Prison duty.
12. Williamston.
13. Hamilton on Roanoke River.
14. Butler's Bridge.
15. Fort Branch.
16. Tarboro.
17. Kinston.
18. South West Creek.
19. Cox's Bridge on Neuse River.
20. Smithfield.
21. Goldsboro.
22. Wilson.

The second document is his obituary, published in the Daily Advance newspaper, in Elizabeth City, North Carolina.

Thirdly, is the United Confederate Veterans Memoriam, given to the families of deceased Camp 1590 members.

A fourth, is a copy of his granddaughter's (Ruth Newbold Vail) application when she joined the United Daughters of the Confederacy.

Illustrations of the Roster pages, obituary, and Memoriam appear in the final chapter.

In examining the original Camp 1590 Roster, it was interesting to see the names of several of grandfather's compatriots who also served in the 68th Regiment. They were; Alex G. Barco, B. F. Bray, Major D. Gregory, William P. Walston, Willoughby D. Gregory, C. B. Morrisette, John C. Perkins, and A. H. Williams. [1]

Discovery of the UCV Memoriam came quite by accident. One day, my wife and I visited the Museum of the Albemarle, near Elizabeth City. At the time, it was a regional museum serving the local community. I asked the attendant if there was a Confederate display, and received a prompt "Yes." We were proudly escorted to a large octagonal glass case, which housed a typical Confederate camp-site.

We worked our way around the display, when suddenly my wife exclaimed, "Come here, and see this."

She was pointing to a wooden pole in the center, upon which were hung various artifacts. What caught her eye, though, was a bundle of papers hanging from a nail. Grandfather William's name, indelibly inscribed in ink, was right on top.

How I eventually acquired this original document, will be described in a later chapter.

Note:
1. Museum of the Albemarle, Elizabeth City, North Carolina

HE BEGINS ANEW

With the war over, and a discharge safely in his pocket, grandfather William made his way home to Camden County. His mother and sister were there to spread the welcome mat. In those early days of spring, he must have contemplated his uncertain future.

Having been a country boy had prepared him to endure the hardships of few comforts, little food, long marches, and the rigours of battle. Youth was in his favor, however, helping him to manage the burden of reconstructing his life. He was destined to live on the land, as a farmer, for the rest of his life.

Before he set his mind to the task at hand, another happy obligation commanded his attention. Gilbert and Charles Grice Elliott, had also returned home to Elizabeth City. A reunion was planned.

Though the cousins were together briefly, in 1861, their trails didn't cross often during the war.

Gilbert, after a respectable time, left Elizabeth City. He became an attorney in New York City. Gilbert died at Fort Wadsworth, New York, on May 9, 1895. His burial was in Green-Wood Cemetery, in Brooklyn, New York. A new Confederate marker now commemorates his former rank and organization (1st Lt.,17th N.C.Regiment), as well as his having been the builder of the C. S. S. Ram Albemarle.[1]

Charles Grice Elliott was eventually an officer of the Atlantic Coast Line railroad. He died while visiting Healing Springs, Virginia, on August 14, 1901. Burial was in Elmwood Cemetery, Norfolk, Virginia. He had been a Captain, Assistant Adjutant General, of the Martin-Kirkland Brigade.[2]

My grandfather's return to the community of Shiloh was, without doubt, a very happy event. The war years had made Camden County a

Notes:

1. The author's application for a V. A. marker, was approved in January, 1988. It was placed on the grave that spring.
2. N.C.Regiments, 1861-1865, by Walter Clark, Vol. IV, pg. 527

haven for the troops of Generals Wild and Butler. The oppression would continue through the post-war military occupation of twelve years. Though the carpetbaggers were in great abundance, at least the fighting was ended. Luckily, the rural areas were able to begin their recovery, with slightly less dominance by the Federals.

I must surmise that William lived with his mother, on property she had purchased from Samuel Upton, on April 29, 1852. The small plot was of about ten acres in area. Perhaps it was an addition to existing property. Samuel Upton described the property as:

> "..beginning at the south corner of Mary Elliott's land at the swamp, thence running in a direct line with her back line to the main road, thence westwardly along said road to the corner of Mary Elliott's land near the garden, thence binding said Mary Elliott's line an eastwardly course to the first station, containing ten acres, be there more or less"... 1

William Harrison Elliott and Martha Jane Duke were married, on December 27, 1865. [2] Martha was the daughter of James Edward Duke and Mary 'Polly' Gray. Mary Gray and her parents, were former residents of Great Bridge, Virginia, before she married James E. Duke.

On December 1, 1866, near the village of Shiloh, in Camden County, the first child, a daughter, was born to William and Martha. They named her Enola Glenn Elliott. Martha died, on August 21, 1882. In 1883 my grandfather moved his family to Perquimans County. It was there, on December 29, 1886, that his first daughter, Enola Glenn Elliott was married to John Newbold.

John, who had been born in 1865, was the son of Henry Clay Newbold and Mary Whitehead.

Notes:

1. Deed Book, AA, pg. 418, Camden County Court House
2. Camden County Marriage Register, 1848-1940

Years ago, a Newbold family member related an anecdote said to be true.

ENOLA ELLIOTT NEWBOLD

"As a young woman, Enola recalled that her father, William, during the winter (probably in 1863), visited his lady-friend, Martha Duke. The story alleged that, after arrival at her home, and once inside the warm house, he had removed his wet boots and long coat, to better enjoy the inviting fireplace. A short time later, the sound of horse hooves could be heard on the road outside.
Martha peeked from the curtains, and saw several Federal cavalry horsemen coming toward the house. William gathered up his coat, bade Martha farewell, and retreated out the back door. At that moment, she noticed his boots on the floor next to the warm hearth. As a knock on the door announced the Federal soldier, she raised her floor-length skirt, stepped into the boots and, dropping her skirt, calmly invited the soldier in. When questioned concerning an alleged Confederate soldier in the area, she pleaded ignorance of the matter, and thus the search-party left." 1

In 1935, John Newbold died at home, near Hertford, North Carolina. Four years later, in 1939, Enola Elliott Newbold was invited to live in Edenton with her daughter, Ruth, and son-in-law, Joseph Matthew Vail. Sixteen years later Enola died, on the 18th of September, 1955, at the age of 88 years and 6 months. Funeral services were conducted at the Holy Trinity Church, in Hertford, with burial in the church yard. Their children were: Ruth Vernon, Martha Eula, Margaret, John Henry, and Mary Elliott Newbold. 2

Notes:

1. Family records of Eula Newbold Greenwood, Kittrell, N. C.
2. Obituary, in December issue, 1955, Episcopal Diocese of N. C.

On August 5, 1869, a second child was born to William and Martha. Sparse records only show the child's name as Charles E. Elliott. Less than two years later, Charles died, on March 27, 1871, in Camden County.

Recovery from the devastation of the war years, while living on a farm with a growing family, was extremely difficult. A mortgage was inevitable:

> "I, William H. Elliott of the County of Camden, in the State of North Carolina,...am indebted to William G. Morrisette of the County in said State, in the sum of sixty dollars,..which he holds my note to be due the first day of January, 1872 and to secure the payment of the same,...I do hereby convey to him this article of property, to wit: All of my growing crop of corn on the farm belonging to N. G. Grandy, when matured...But on this special trust that if I fail to pay said debt and interest on or before the first day of January, 1872, then he said Morrisette may sell said corn or so much thereof as may be necessary by public auction for cash, first giving twenty days notice at three public places and apply the proceeds of such sale to the discharge of said debt and..interest on the same and pay any surplus to me. Given under my hand and seal this 13th day of May, 1871." 1

For the first time, William is known to be farming on property other than his own. I found no further entries at the Camden Court House concerning the mortgage of May 13, 1871. Thus, it appears William retired the note before January 1, 1872, as promised.

His sister, Mary Jane ("Mollie") Elliott, married Joseph S. Walston, in Camden County, on December 14, 1871. The Walston's have remained within Camden County as prominent farmers, businessmen, and law enforcement officers.

Note:
1. Deed Book, DD, pg. 51, Camden County Court House

Mary Elliott Walston, grandfather's sister, died on May 10, 1916, and was buried in the cemetery across from the Shiloh Church.

The third child of William and Martha, was a daughter. She was named Mary Matilda Elliott. 'Tilla', as she was always to be known, was born on June 16, 1872, in Camden County, near Shiloh.

Later she was married to Daniel Sawyer, on June 11, 1904.

After residing a few years in Norfolk, Virginia, they moved to their final home in Washington, D. C. Tilla died there, on March 5, 1953, at age 71. Their children were: Dorothy E., and Richard Leigh Sawyer.

MARY ELLIOTT SAWYER

William and Martha's fourth child was a son, whom they named John Pool Elliott. He was born near Shiloh, in Camden County, on April 3, 1875. On October 24, 1904, John Pool (known as 'Jack'), married Myrtis Myrick. The Myrick family were industrious farmers near Littleton, North Carolina.

After the marriage, Jack and Myrtis moved to Richmond, Virginia, where they raised their family. When, in later years, Jack was asked about his recollections of his grandmother, Mary Brockett Elliott, he could only recall that when he was age 10, he attended her funeral in Camden County. He further observed it was 'so sad.' The only other memory, of the occasion was of seeing so many windmills in the country area where the funeral took place. In later years, the windmill area was identified as being along the east shore of

JOHN POOL ELLIOTT

the Pasquotank River, just west of Shiloh. To some, it has been known as Texaco Shores.

John Pool Elliott had a career in the lumber business, real estate, and merchandising. He died in Richmond, on May 25, 1963, and his wife Myrtis died, on May 28, 1967. Both are buried in Calvary Church cemetery near Littleton, North Carolina. Their children were: Enola Catharine, John Pool Jr., Myrtis, Marion ('Polly') Hill, and James Duke Elliott.

From the time 'Mollie' Elliott had married Joseph S. Walston, 1n 1871, until sometime in 1876, Joe Walston evidently allowed William to use a portion of his extensive property, for the purpose of raising a crop. Grandfather again experienced a shortage of cash, while he waited for the fall crop to mature. A second loan was necessary:

"I, William H. Elliott of Camden County, State of North Carolina, am indebted to T. H. Jorden and Bros., in the sum of forty dollars for which they hold my note to be due the first day of December, 1875, and to secure the payment of the same, I do hereby convey to them these articles of personal property, to wit: My entire crop of corn now being cultivated on the lands of Joseph S. Walston. But on this special trust that if I fail to pay said debt on or before the first day of December, 1875, then they may sell said property, or so much thereof as may be necessary, for cash,..first giving twenty days notice at three public places and apply the proceeds of such sale to the discharge of said debt and pay any surplus to me. Given under my hand and seal this 9th day of July, 1875" 1

Note:
1. Deed Book, EE, pg. 500, Camden County Court House

Expected prosperity evidently failed to materialize, because the next year he repeated the borrowing process:

"I, William H. Elliott..of the County and State aforesaid am indebted to Grandy Williams and Co., of Norfolk, Virginia in the sum of fifty dollars for which they hold my note due the first day of December, 1876 with interest at 8% per annum from date until paid and to secure the payment of same I do hereby convey to them the following articles of personal property, to wit: One bay mare named Kate, and all of my crop of corn and cotton raised during the year 1876 on land rented of Joseph S. Walston. But on this special trust that if I fail to pay said debt and interest..on or before the first day of December, 1876, then they may sell said property or so much thereof as may be necessary at public auction for cash, first giving ten days notice at three public places and apply the proceeds of such sale..to the discharge of said debt and interest on same and pay any surplus to me. Given under my hand and seal this 24th day of May, 1876"... 1

It's interesting to note the increase in terms required by the lender. In addition to the crop, the lender charged 8% interest, held the mare 'Kate', and limited the foreclosure notice to ten days.

The last of five children of grandfather William and Martha, was a third son. He was born on August 28, 1877, in Camden County, and they named him William Thomas Duke Elliott.

William T. D. Elliott only knew his mother for the first five years of his life, as she died in 1882.

He attended the rural district schools as a boy, and later went to Hertford Academy, North Carolina. Much later, he attended the University of Buffalo, New York, from which he graduated in law. Returning to North Carolina, he passed the bar exams, and practised law within the State. During his years in college, he married Arletta Snyder, of Buffalo, New York, on January 17, 1905.

Note:
1. Deed Book, FF, pg. 175, Camden County Court House

WILLIAM T. D. ELLIOTT

In 1908, William Thomas Duke Elliott, and his wife, moved to Rochester, New York. His Elliott Realty Company was located in the old Granite Building, at 130 Main Street. In Easter week of 1911, Joseph Keaton Elliott, his young brother, joined the real estate firm as a partner.

In mid-December, 1922, William T. D. Elliott became ill. He succumbed to pneumonia, on the 23rd of December, 1922, at his home in Rochester. Burial was in Forest Lawn Cemetery in Buffalo. Their children were: Harriet, and William T. D. Elliott, Jr.

There can be little doubt that rural life, and the concerns of raising a family, took it's toll on Martha Duke Elliott, for she died on August 21, 1882. Although no headstone has been located, it appears reasonable that Martha was buried in the Shiloh Church cemetery, as William was carried on the roll as a member in 1882.

Despondent over this tragic event, and worried that farming had become unprofitable, William packed up his family, and his mother, Mary Brockett Elliott, and moved to Perquimans County. I'm guessing they settled near Hertford. Though no exact date of their move has been found, they were in Perquimans by late 1883, or early 1884.

William's mother, Mary, the daughter of John A. Brockett, of Camden County, had a sister, Lydia. Lydia was married to John Burgess. They had a son, John Burgess, Jr., who then married Virginia E. Newbold. 'Jennie', as she was thereafter known, was born on October 17, 1847.

Early in 1884, William's first cousin, John Burgess, Jr., died. After a reasonable time, William married John's widow, Jennie, the daughter of James and Mary E. Newbold, of Perquimans County. Rev. O. C. Horton, a Perquimans Baptist Minister, performed the ceremony at the residence of V. E. Burgess, on April 30, 1884.[1] The Burgess family lived in the tiny community of Parksville, about eight miles northeast of Hertford. Three witnesses who signed the Marriage Register were K. R. Newbold, W. N. Newbold, and C. F. Sumner, all of Perquimans County.

William and Jennie later had one daughter, who died an infant. Virginia 'Jennie' died, on October 25, 1884. A reference is made to the burial of a Jennie Burgess in Salem Baptist Church Yard, in Pasquotank County.[2] The birth and death dates are seemingly correct, but her married name 'Elliott' is omitted. Could she be the second wife of grandfather William?

It was only natural that my grandfather would become very despondent over the death of Jennie. His grief was compounded by the fact that his children were again motherless.

When word of Jennie's death reached Mollie Walston, she promptly wrote her brother to convey her sorrow, and guide his spirit to accept the inevitable.

Original letters were recovered from grandfather's family by my mother, Edna Garrison Elliott. They suggest that Mollie Walston, and her brother William, shared a very close understanding of each other. Mollie seemed to be of a very religious nature. Excerpts of several of her letters substantiate this view:

Notes:

1. Perquimans County Marriage Register, Vol. I, 1852-1940
2. Tombstones & Epitaphs of Northeastern North Carolina, pg. 225, 'Salem Baptist Church Yard Burials,' by Wilma Cartwright Spence

"My Dearest Brother   Dec. 11, 1884

 I received the postal Tuesday just before eleven
o'clock. Duty demands an answer, but I do feel as
if I could not write. How can I write, so sad, so
full of trouble, my heart aches for you. I feel
inadequate to express my sorrow, my sympathy for
you. I was in hope that..I should hear that she
was better. Dear brother you must bear it the very
best you can. I know it is hard to bear, but as
she told me in her letter informing me of little
Jennie's death that she knew that the "Lord love-
eth Whome He Chastneth," that it was all for the
best. I know if she could speak from the spirit
world she would say,...'grieve not for me.' "

      I am your loving sister

       Mollie J. Walston

 Mollie's mention of 'little Jennie's death,'..seems to say the
baby had also been named Jennie.

 Family recollections, and the contents of Mollie Walston's next
letter to her brother William, dated January 13, reveal that Mary
Brockett Elliott, their mother, was then in Camden County. She had
made the trip between late December, 1884, and early January, 1885.

 About one month after her first letter, Mollie again wrote her
brother:

   "My Dear Brother   Jan. 13, 1885

 It affords me pleasure to write to you this morning, and feel that it will give you the same to
receive it. I do hope by this time you are feeling
better in mind although I know you are none the
less lonely...I know you miss her in the church
and at the piano and all those lessons of instruction put up by her for your benefit...Brother you
must give it up, make up your mind to do so at once
be strengthened by God...take care of your debts,
do not let anything escape you..I think I would
sell those logs you have if you can. I know for
what purpose you got them, you wanted to please
her..hoping you will not think hard of me for so
doing, for I know you are a poor man and are responsible for a great deal now..was glad to see
mother. Mother says if you can, send her some wool

to knit some socks for you and the children. She was sorry she forgot it."

I am your devoted sister

Mollie J. Walston

The January 13th letter portrays the increasingly dire financial straits into which William was falling. Remorse over the death of Jennie was becoming too great a burden.

One month later to the day, Mollie again wrote to William:

"My Dear Brother   Feb. 13, 1885

I thought I would not put off...writing to you any longer for I know...you are beginning to be anxious to hear from us as we are always to hear from you. We have had bitter cold weather. Today it is cold and rainy. Such days are always dull and lonely causing us to appreciate more highly the bright sunny days. Mr. Mathias Garenton died last week, had been down a long time with consumption. Was willing to die, said the angels was with him and all around him. At one time he told his wife that the Savior had been to him, said he was sorry she was asleep when He came....Mr. Wilder went over to Perquimans, but we did not know of his going, if so we would have written to you and sent by him. Mr. Duke came to see us not long ago to hear from you all. He is well and fat as ever. He is very sorry for you, would like to go to see you but it will cost him too much on the train, he lives with Mr. Dozier yet....Tell Nola, they did not have Lillie Sanderlins love scrap up in church as was expected. They want it to drop if possible. Johnathon Brockett lives at Mr. Morrisettes place at Shiloh, he lives down stairs... Mother is well, sitting in the corner wrapped up in her shawl as it is so cool. She wants to know how you all are and what you are doing. Yes Bud, little Billie is delicate now but he may be stronger as he grows older. I would not compel him to go to school when it is real cold..Johnnie is a good child. I was so glad that you have noticed how easily managed he is and his disposition also is good."...

Your devoted sister

Mollie Walston

The mention that Mr. Wilder had gone to Perquimans County, and could have personally carried a letter, indicates that grandfather William and his four children, were residing in Perquimans County at the time.

Judging from the tenor of Mollie's March 6th letter, William's morale was elevated, and he was beginning to experience improvement in his financial affairs:

> "My Dear Brother   March 6, 1885
>
> ..we were glad to hear that you were well, I am not very well today, have had an attack of earache, my head roars and feels badly. I was glad to know you have arranged your business, hope you can sell your mule to advantage soon, but as you say, money is scarce..your spelling class is very good, will learn the children a great deal...Mr. Duke came in while I was writing, was compelled to stop.. Bud have you sown your garden yet. Joe and I have sown ours, planted peas, beets, potatoes, etc. I told you all, must keep a part of this paper to say a few words to Nola...Mother sends her best love to you and the children, she is well and sitting in the corner, thinking no doubt of you all."
>
>   Your loving sister
>
>   Mollie J. Walston

Mary Brockett Elliott remained with Mollie and Joseph Walston, and died in their home, on July 27, 1885, at the age of 73 years, 5 months. One can only imagine the great sense of loss and mourning by William and Mollie. Mary had, in reality, lived two roles, that of a father, and as a loving mother. She had taught William to be an honest man, calm of nature, charitable, and forgiving. Her firm faith in God was often reflected by her son Williams' actions.

Though the war years had been rigorous, no remark from any of his children, nor his last wife, Dorothy Keaton Elliott, my grandmother, ever suggested the war had left emotional scars.

Sometime after the death of Mary Brockett Elliott, and the early spring of 1886, grandfather returned with the children, to Pasquotank County. He established residence near Nixonton.

Grandfather had formerly known John and Dorothy Price, of Nix-
onton. They were married in Nixonton, on February 13, 1870. One witness had been her brother, Joseph Z. Keaton.

After two children were born, the father and youngsters became
ill with fever, and died. Dorothy was left alone in her small frame
house, in the center of the village of Nixonton. Inevitably, William renewed his acquaintance with the widow of John Price.

WILLIAM HARRISON ELLIOTT and DOROTHY KEATON ELLIOTT
1886

That spring (1886), my grandfather proposed marriage, and Dorothy
accepted. The prospect of marrying a man with four children was not
an unusual circumstance in the society of that era. In the home of
the bride, Rev. Josiah Elliott, Minister of the Gospel, performed the
marriage ceremony, uniting William H. Elliott, and Dorothy 'Dolly'
Keaton Price, on April 1, 1886. The groom was 45 years old, and the
bride was 34. Dorothy's birthday was May 25, 1851. How fortunate it
was that a photographer was present for the occasion.

The new bride began housekeeping with her ready-made family of four children. She met the challenge well. Enola, eldest daughter of William, was now 20, and would be married within seven months. Daughter Tilla was now 14. Son Jack was 11, and the youngest son, William T. D., was 9.

The location of William H. Elliott's house on Symond Creek, in 1886, is shown by the arrow.

AMBITIONS REALIZED

Since his return from Perquimans County, my grandfather had been looking for farm property on which to settle. He found a house and some land to rent at Symond Creek, about 2 or 3 miles east of Nixonton. The house was on the west side of the creek, about fifteen hundred feet south of the highway bridge. Today, only a rock pile marks the foundation site.

The year 1886 proved to be a landmark year for grandfather. He had moved from Perquimans County in April. He was married for the third time. He started a new home and planted his crops. He gave his eldest daughter, Enola, to John Newbold in marriage, on December 29th. For the ceremony his family traveled back to Perquimans, where the groom lived.

January of 1887 proved to be another eventful month. On the 18th, the first child of William and Dorothy was born at their Symond Creek home. They named their son, Joseph Keaton Elliott.

In 1907, Joe left the farm, with his parent's blessing. He went to join elder brother, Jack, in Littleton, nearly 115 miles west. After he learned the lumber business from Joseph Z. Keaton, Jack had developed a large clientele, which provided employment opportunity for Joe. A year later, in 1908, Joe was buying logs near Halifax, about 30 miles to the east of Littleton. A lumber broker in Norfolk bought the logs. Joe stayed on the job, until 1911. At that time, William T. D.,

JOSEPH KEATON ELLIOTT

Joe's other brother, was studying North Carolina law, to take the State Bar exams. During one of their sporadic visits, Bill and Joe agreed to organize a partnership in real estate sales, where Bill lived, in Rochester, New York.

By Easter week, of 1911, Joe had arrived in Rochester. Within a year, a friend introduced Joe to a young lady, Edna Mae Garrison. After a most lengthy courtship, Joe and Edna were married, on the 21st of April, 1915. I am the only child of Joe and Edna.

When dad was 78, he and my mother chose to retire to St. Petersburg, Florida. There they resided in comfortable retirement, until he died, on June 26, 1978, at age 91. Edna preferred to remain in her home at St. Petersburg. While recuperating from illness at age 94, she died in Daytona Beach, on April 9, 1984. Both she and dad are buried in St. Petersburg's Memorial Park.

My dad, Joseph K. Elliott, was a Mason, and a member of the Sons of The American Revolution. He also was a member of the Sons of Confederate Veterans, and the Military Order of the Stars and Bars (A Society of Male Descendants of the Military and Governmental leadership of the Confederate States of America). He was recognized as a REAL SON of a Confederate Veteran.

Grandfather seemed destined not only to live on rented land, but also to till the same soil. Surely he harbored a dream of one day being a landowner. This dream would not become a reality, however, for several more years.

In his later years, dad recalled that his father kept the family at Symond Creek, for a little less than a year. They then moved northward to the Charles farm, about three miles from Elizabeth City. This was to be their home for nearly three years, from late 1887 to late 1890.

On January 5, 1888, grandfather paid his 1886 tax bill, a total of $1.76. This covered the short time he was in Pasquotank County, after having moved from Perquimans County.

No. 77

NIXONTON TOWNSHIP

Pasquotank Co., N. C., _Jan 5th_ 1888

Received of _Wm E Elliott_

One 76/100 Dollars,

in full payment of County Taxes for 1886:

State Tax,	$ 75
County Tax,	1.01
Poll Tax,	
Total,	$ 1.76

W D Cohun Sheriff.

EDWARDS, BROUGHTON & CO., STEAM PRINTERS AND BINDERS, RALEIGH.

No. 95

NIXONTON TOWNSHIP,

PASQUOTANK CO., N. C., _Jan 5th_ 1889

Received of _W. H. Elliott_

Five 9/100 Dollars,

in full payment of County Taxes for 1888:

State Tax,	$ 60
School Tax,	38
County Tax,	1.03
Court-House Tax,	1.08
Poll Tax,	2.00
Total,	$ 5.09

F H Cohun Sheriff.

EDWARDS & BROUGHTON, PRINTERS AND BINDERS, RALEIGH.

A year later, on January 5, 1889, he paid his taxes for the year 1888, when he was on the Charles farm. This time, the total had risen to $5.09. The county had added a School Tax, and a Court House Tax.

STATE OF NORTH CAROLINA,
PASQUOTANK COUNTY.

I, William H. Elliott of Nixonton Township of the County and State aforesaid, am indebted to _Guirkin &_ _(Bankers)_ of said County in said sum of _Twenty Seven & 30/100 Dollars ($27.30)_ for which they hold my note, to be due the _6th_ day of _November_ 1889 ; and to secure the payment of the same, I do hereby convey to _C. Guirkin_ as Trustee, these articles of personal property, to-wit :

My entire growing crop of Cotton, Corn & Rice, cultivated by me on the lands I rent of T. L. Sanderson, known as the Chanba farm - Situated in Township County, & State aforesaid - Say 15 m in Cotton 150 m in Corn & 6 m in Rice

But on this special trust, that if I fail to pay said debt and interest. on or before the _6th_ day of _November_ 1889, then the said _C. Guirkin_ Trustee, may sell said property, or so much thereof as may be necessary, by public auction, for cash, first giving twenty days' notice at three public places, and appl. the proceeds of such sale to the discharge of said debt and interest on the same, due _Guirkin & Co- (Bankers)_, and pay any surplus to me.

Given under our hands and seals, this _6th_ day of _July_ A. D. 1889.

Executed in presence of

M. R. Culpepper   Wm. H. Elliott {Seal}

                         C. Guirkin Trustee {Seal}

It was while on the Charles farm that grandfather William signed for another loan, on July 6, 1889. My dad, Joseph, told me that
the reason for the loan was, not only to procure planting seed for
a fall crop, but also for a supply of household staples. The crop
matured favorably, and was sold on time. From the profit, William
paid off the note which was due, on November 6, 1889.

Twelve days after the note was to have been due, the second child,
a daughter, was born to William and Dorothy, on November, 18, 1889.
They named her Sarah Berry Elliott.
Her half sister, Tilla, then age 17,
was to prove most helpful to Dorothy,
in caring for younger Sarah over the
next five years. On the 27th of October, 1915, Miss Sarah was married to
William C. Myrick, in Littleton. The
couple made their permanent home just
east of town, in the country. William
Myrick spent his life-time as a farmer and country merchant. On the 11th
of February, 1963, William died. His
wife Sarah died after a lengthy illness, on October 15, 1974. Both are
buried near their home, in the Calvary Church cemetery. The two children of William and Sarah were: Dorothy Kathryn and William C. Myrick, Jr.

SARAH BERRY ELLIOTT

Always seeking an improvement opportunity, grandfather again moved his
family back to Nixonton, in 1891 or
1892. He rented the Bright house, located south of the main street,
near the Little River. Dorothy's old frame house, now vacant, was
one block east from the school at the corner, where the main road

turned at a right angle, into the village. The Bright house was to be their residence for about a year.

In 1892, grandfather moved the family a few hundred yards to the Cartwright house, on the north side of the main street, in the center of Nixonton. They lived there for another year.

William and Dorothy became parents of their third child, on August 21, 1892. A daughter, she was named Lucy Marie Elliott. The sisters, Lucy and Sarah, grew up on their father's farms, and as they became older, they assumed a number of household responsibilities. At the age of 20, in 1912, Lucy married Nix Morgan, of Elizabeth City. After the death of Nix Morgan in 1941, Lucy then married Eugene C. Bobbitt, who died seven years later in 1948. For many years afterward, Lucy resided with her daughter and son-in-law, Marie and Herman Eley, in Franklin, Virginia. She would later make her home at the Hopewell Convalescent Center in Hopewell, Virginia.

LUCY MARIE ELLIOTT

Lucy Marie Bobbitt was honored when the City Point Chapter, United Daughters of the Confederacy, presented her with a REAL DAUGHTER medal with certificate. At their regular meeting, on April 25, 1979, Chapter members made the Sons of Confederate Veterans award, with party festivities, at the convalescent center. Lucy's companions in residence were all party guests.

On March 25, 1980, Lucy died, at age 88. She was buried in New Hollywood Cemetery, in Elizabeth City. The children of Nix and Lucy Morgan were: Charles Elliott, and Sarah Marie Morgan.

By 1893, William had again moved eastward, to a rural area known as the 'Glade,' where they lived on another rented farm for about a year.

Since 1871, grandfather had been living on rented farms. His two older sons, John Pool and William T. Duke, helped greatly in tending crops, and handling their share of the farm chores, when they were not in school.

Late in 1894, grandfather William moved his family onto another rented farm. The house was a huge two-story frame structure, with the characteristic veranda on the front.

One July day in 1975, my father, Joseph Keaton Elliott, and I, were standing in the front yard of this last rented farm of grandfather William. We had spent the day driving around south-central Pasquotank County, visiting those old areas where grandfather had lived, after his marriage to Dorothy Keaton Price.

We were facing the quiet pavement, known as Body Road. Looking left we could see what dad had known as Persimmon Tree corner. Shading his eyes from the sun, while gazing toward the corner, he exclaimed:

> "When we were kids, late in May,....on a Sunday afternoon after church, we used to go to this.. field to eat strawberries. We'd just lie down and eat and eat till we were stuffed. Then, on Monday mornings when Papa would have us hoe cotton, or corn, I'd be so sick I couldn't work. Papa often wondered why this happened. One time he learned the reason and we were caught. He never really punished us, we just couldn't go out for a while on Sunday afternoons."

Glancing toward the house to our rear, and then pointing across the road, dad continued:

> "For a rented farm, it had been a good size for those days. I guess there must have been nearly one hundred forty acres. The property was located on both sides of the road. Opposite the house was a large woods, as now, through which a wagon

path led to a large cultivated field beyond. It
was there that I spent many hours tending crops,
when not in school...which was less than a mile
distant."

Dad was about seven years old when they moved into this larger
house, and his job was:

"...to chop weeds in the fields, plant seeds or
carry fire wood to the kitchen. As I grew older,
Papa would allow me to drive the horse a little
at a time."

Less than a mile south of this farm on Body Road was a road to
the right. Dad and I drove to that right turn, and stopped in front
of the Halls Creek Methodist Church. As we stood by the roadside,
he seemed to be remembering out loud:

"The church we went to usually, was right here.
It was only about a half mile walk. Our regular
church was at Woodville, some four miles northwest, too far to walk. We had only one horse, who
had to do all the heavy farm work, and Papa believed in letting her rest on Sundays. Once every
quarter though, the family did attend church in
Woodville, and to drive the family,..Papa would
make the Saturday before, an easier work day for
the horse. Papa had been Clerk of the Woodville
Baptist Church. His first records began in Book
Number 2, in 1888."

As we walked west from the church, dad and I stopped on the Halls
Creek bridge. The scene stirred more memories of his youth:

"One time, in the winter (1895), we were in the
wagon going to our empty tenant house..to check
our drying peanuts. Peanuts grow attached to the
roots under the soil, like potatoes. We would pull
the stalks and pile them loosely to dry.
This particular morning we planned to pick off
the dry peanuts. There was Papa, Jack, and me.
Jack was most grown by then, probably about 20
years old. It must have been about 1895,...as we
had been living on the nearby farm over a year.
Our one mare was pulling the wagon. We had left
her colt back in the barn, but he became panicky
when he saw her trotting off down the road,...so

he kicked his gate out and ran after us. Papa said
'it was all right' when the colt came running up
along side.

Halls Creek was covered with ice that time of
year, and as we drove across on the bridge, that
colt decided he would run across on the ice. When
he got out away from the bank, his weight caused
the thin ice to begin sinking. Jack had seen what
was going to happen, so he had jumped off the wagon and ran down the bank. He grabbed an old fence
post and began breaking the ice out as far as he
could reach. Then, spotting a row boat on the bank
nearby, he skidded it out before him, and reached
the colt just as he was going under. Jack grabbed
an ear to hold his head above water, while they
made their way back to the bank.

Papa, in the meantime, had driven to the other
side of the bridge, and was yelling for help. A
few houses nearby were filled with his friends,
and before you knew it, a crowd had gathered.

Jack, by then, had a hold of the colt's halter,
and himself in the water, was trying to get the
colt's feet on solid bottom. When Jack got him
out, Papa told me, 'Well, he'll catch cold after
being in that water, Joe, you take him home and
dry him off'..so I got a piece of rope from the
wagon, tied it to his halter, and we started out
along the road for home. I was right pleased about
it all, as I didn't want to pick off the peanuts
anyway.

Down the road a way was a puddle, and try as I
would, I couldn't make that colt walk through the
water,..he just swung way out around it, staying
on dry ground. Back at the barn I gave him a good
rub down, put a blanket on him,..and locked the
stable. Next day he was fine as ever."

I asked where dad's brother Bill was when the colt broke through
the ice, and dad said:

"Bill had already left home. probably to attend
school at the Hertford Academy, or to visit his
sister Enola Newbold."

Sometime in 1895, grandfather William began making plans to buy
his own farm. For years the family had lived on rented properties,
and had moved about the country a number of times, never having a
permanent home.

Grandfather knew of some property, on Body Road, closer to Nixonton. There was no house, but that didn't bother him, at all. He had an idea. He would put a ready-made house on the land. He had saved enough for the purchase price. But first, before the house was built, a barn must be raised to house the livestock and store the feed.

Grandfather achieved his dream of becoming a member of the landed gentry, on January 31, 1896. The momentous event in described in a condensed version of the Deed:

> "William H. Elliott buys from Richard Barden and wife Margaret of Perquimans County for a sum of $200.00, a parcel of land..in Nixonton Township adjoining the lands of James Banks, Simon Granberry and others, bounded as follows; Lying on the road leading from Nixonton to Elizabeth City, adjoining the lands formerly belonging to the heirs of Mary Overman and the heirs of Thomas Davis, deceased, and being the same tract of land which the said Barden purchased from George W. Jackson and wife, which Deed is recorded in Book SS, page 56, Pasquotank County, said tract being 28 acres." 1

Again, I encouraged dad's memory of the occasion, by asking him to relate how grandfather acquired the house:

> "Papa decided to move Mama's house from Nixonton. After they had been married in 1886,...the house had stood vacant. In the meantime,...we had been going to the farm and getting the land ready in the spring of 1896. This new farm was only half way between the two-story farm house..we had in 1895, and Nixonton. We worked all year getting in a crop of corn, stock peas, and some cotton.
> When it came time to harvest the crop and stack the fodder, a neighbor across the road told Papa he could use a space near the road,..which Papa did. Papa had hired a man he knew, who owned two yokes of oxen, to move Mama's little house. He used two-inch thick oak planks with rollers,...which allowed the oxen to move it a little at a time. With hard wood rollers, the half mile trip didn't

Note:
1.Deed Book 17, pgs. 61,62 Pasquotank County Court House

> take long at all. When the end of the planks were
> reached in front, the oxen were stopped, and the
> rear planks were brought forward...to make more
> hard surface for the rollers. Papa had selected
> an exact spot he wanted for the house,...and it
> was most sundown when it was located properly.
>   I guess the man must have stayed there all night
> or he tied the oxen and went home, anyway, during
> the night they smelled the fodder across the road
> and broke their tethers.
>   By morning, when Papa saw them, the fodder stack
> was most gone. Papa's first comment was, 'Lordy,
> whatever will I do for feed now?'...thinking of
> his horse and a few cows. In reply, the owner of
> the oxen said, 'Uncle Billy, don't you fret none,
> it won't hurt them a bit.' Papa could only smile
> at that and the matter was passed off."

Perhaps his war experience had taught grandfather not to worry
about circumstances beyond his control. With just a few more words,
dad concluded the tale of the house-moving:

> "As soon as the house was anchored firmly on the
> rock foundation, we moved right in, early in 1897.
> Papa, Jack, and I built on three new rooms. The
> kitchen and dining room were on the back of the
> house, and we made an extra room upstairs. In our
> first year there, Papa and I had planted two oak
> trees in the front yard. After that we enclosed
> the whole yard with a white fence and gate."

On January 17, 1897, their fourth child was born to William and
Dorothy. A son, they named him Roy F. Elliott. Sadly, he died on the
25th of July, 1897, and was buried in a family plot. A headstone
marks the grave. The small cemetery had been established by a former owner, in the southwest corner of the farm, near the woods line.

This Elliott section was eventually enclosed by a wrought-iron
fence, with the compliments of Nix Morgan.

Several months after grandfather William had settled on his new
farm, his first son, Jack, decided to leave home. During 1890, my
grandmother Dorothy's brother, Joseph Z. Keaton, offered to teach
Jack the lumber business, if Jack would come and work for him. Jack

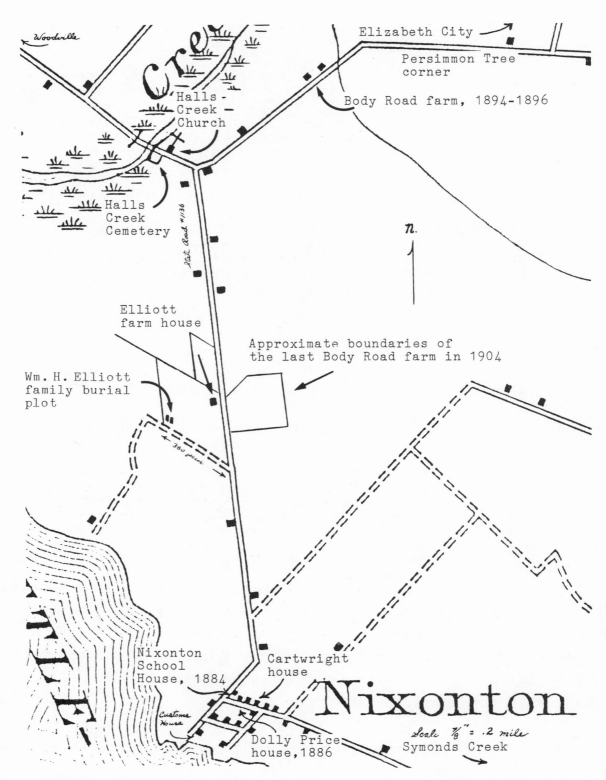

Woodville

Elizabeth City

Persimmon Tree corner

Body Road farm, 1894-1896

Halls-Creek-Church

Halls Creek Cemetery

n.

Elliott farm house

Approximate boundaries of the last Body Road farm in 1904

Wm. H. Elliott family burial plot

380 poles

Nixonton School House, 1884

Cartwright house

Customs House

Nixonton

Dolly Price house, 1886

Scale ⅞" = .2 mile

Symonds Creek

William Elliott's last farm and home nearly one mile north of Nixonton, N.C.

remained with his uncle, Joe Keaton, for about a year. His job required business visits to Norfolk, Elizabeth City, and Littleton. Lumber brokers in Norfolk bought the rough-cut timber. It was while working in and around Littleton, that Jack became acquainted with the Myrick family. A daughter, Myrtis Myrick, later became his wife.

With the loss of Jack's help, grandfather noticed the additional strain of working the farm with fewer hands. By 1901, a succession of profitable crops permitted grandfather to consider an addition to his farm. He purchased a small parcel of from 4 to 6 acres for $25.00. The transaction was completed on January 1, 1901. In somewhat condensed form, the Deed specified:

> "William H. Elliott buys from John S. Morris and wife Ada for a sum of $25.00, a parcel of land in Nixonton Township adjoining lands of W. H. Elliott and Mary Overton and others, bounded as follows:
> Commencing at ditch at James Banks line and running a southeasterly course down W. H. Elliott's line about five hundred and seventy feet to the corner of Morris lead ditch that runs to swamp, thence down said ditch west about...two hundred and sixty feet to an old ditch parallel with line first mentioned; thence down said old ditch about five hundred and seventy feet to said Banks line, thence east along said line about two hundred.. and seventy feet to place of beginning, making a piece of land from 4 to 6 acres, being a part of George Davis land." 1

The year 1904 brought another addition of acreage consisting of a 17 acre plot across the road from William's prospering small farm. He closed the purchase on June 1, 1904. This abbreviated Deed description states that:

> "..William H. Elliott buys from Will and Israel Lister and Alma Overman of Pasquotank County, for a sum of $125.00, a parcel of land..in Nixonton Township, adjoining the lands of Joseph Harrell, deceased, and others, bounded as follows:

Note:
1.Deed Book 24, pgs. 295, 296   Pasquotank County Court House

On the north by the lands of...Joseph Harrell, deceased, on the east by John S. Morris, on the south by a public road and on the west by public road, on the northwest by...the lands of Elijah Overton, deceased, containing 17 acres."... 1

A witness to this Deed was Joseph Keaton Elliott. The Deed was proven before W. H. Jennings, Clerk of Superior Court, and registered by J. C. Spence, Registrar of Deeds, on August 26, 1908, in Pasquotank County.

In 1905, grandfather William at the age of 64, allowed his son Joseph to be virtual owner and manager of the farm. By such an act grandfather reduced his personal level of responsibility...in the twilight of his years. For two years thereafter, Joe operated the farm, until he left home, in 1907, to join his brother Jack. Joe didn't depart, however, until August that year, after the crops had been harvested. Though many miles separated Joe from his father and mother, while he was working in northeastern North Carolina, he was able to return frequently to visit and assist grandfather about the farm.

Note:
1. Deed Book 32, pgs. 213,214   Pasquotank County Court House

THE ELLIOTT FARM HOUSE ON BODY ROAD, CIRCA 1910

Appearing left to right: my grandfather, William Harrison Elliott; grandmother, Dorothy Keaton Elliott; with daughters, Lucy Marie, and Sarah Berry Elliott.

On the following pages are photographs including each of grandfather's children in their later years. Although in several cases each family member is not represented, nevertheless these are the most representative that could be found.

ENOLA ELLIOTT NEWBOLD and JOHN NEWBOLD,
with her nephew and niece,
WILLIAM THOMAS DUKE ELLIOTT, JR., and HARRIETT ELLIOTT
CIRCA, 1911

DANIEL and
TILLA ELLIOTT SAWYER
WASHINGTON, D.C.
CIRCA, 1932

JOHN POOL ELLIOTT and MYRTIS MYRICK ELLIOTT,
with youngest son, JAMES DUKE ELLIOTT, in front;
daughters MYRTIS, and MARION (POLLY) ELLIOTT,
EDNA GARRISON ELLIOTT, and JOHN POOL ELLIOTT, JR.
RICHMOND, VA.
CIRCA, 1937

WILLIAM THOMAS DUKE ELLIOTT and ARLETTA SNYDER ELLIOTT,
son WILLIAM T. D. ELLIOTT, JR., and daughter, HARRIETT ELLIOTT
ROCHESTER, N.Y.
CIRCA, 1920

JOSEPH KEATON ELLIOTT and
EDNA GARRISON ELLIOTT, left;
son, ROBERT GARRISON ELLIOTT,
and JOSEPH'S mother, DOROTHY
KEATON ELLIOTT.
          SYRACUSE, N. Y.
               1931

          SARAH ELLIOTT MYRICK,
with son, WILLIAM CLEMENTS
MYRICK, JR., and daughter,
DOROTHY KATHRYN MYRICK
          LITTLETON, N. C.
               1923

NIX MORGAN, LUCY ELL-
IOTT MORGAN, and EDNA
GARRISON ELLIOTT.
  Left Front, CHARLES
ELLIOTT MORGAN, SARAH
MARIE MORGAN, and ROB-
ERT GARRISON ELLIOTT.
ELIZABETH CITY, N.C.
       1922

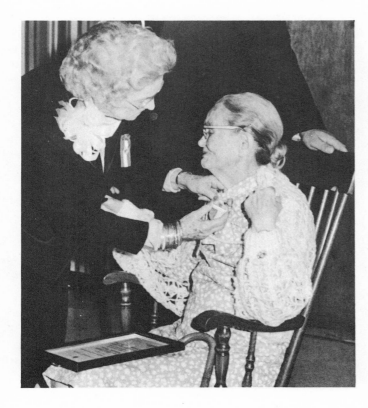

LUCY ELLIOTT MORGAN BOBBITT
receives SONS of CONFEDERATE
VETERANS, REAL DAUGHTER MEDAL
from MRS. W. W. CLEERE, PRES.
the City Point Chapter, Virginia, United Daughters of the
Confederacy, at her UDC membership induction ceremony.
     HOPEWELL, VIRGINIA
       APRIL, 1979

Joseph Keaton Elliott, 90, was recognized as a REAL SON of a Confederate Veteran on Saturday, March 5, 1977. The presentation was made during the Charter ceremony of the James F. Hull Camp 1347, Sons of Confederate Veterans, in Daytona Beach, Florida.

My mother, Edna Garrison Elliott, shared the proud moment with my dad, as they were photographed the next morning. The Sons of Confederate Veterans lapel pin, the Military Order of the Stars and Bars minature medal, and REAL SON medal, were worn by my father as symbols of deep respect and admiration for the Confederate service of his father, Lt. William Harrison Elliott.

A VETERAN RECOGNIZED

Many of grandfather William's former army comrades still lived in Pasquotank, and neighboring Camden County. After repeated words of encouragement, he considered joining the William F. Martin Camp 1590, United Confederate Veterans, in Elizabeth City. During the August 11, 1909-1910 annual meeting, grandfather William, and several old comrades-in-arms became members of Camp 1590.[1]

What may be the most comprehensive review of the William F. Martin Camp 1590, was composed by William W. Forehand of Shiloh.

WILLIAM F. MARTIN
CAMP   1590
'UNITED CONFEDERATE VETERANS'

by W. W. Forehand

"A few years after the Civil War had ended, the veterans of that War in the South,....formed an organization, naming it,....'United Confederate Veterans,' with Headquarters, or Grand Camp, in New Orleans.
The object, or purpose, of the organization was strictly social, literary, benevolent, and historical. It endeavored to unite a general federation of associations..of Confederate veteran soldiers now in existence,...or hereafter to be found, to gather authentic data for an impartial history of the War between the States, to preserve relics or mementoes of the same, to cherish the ties of friendship that should exist..among men who have shared common dangers, common sufferings, and privations, to care for all the disabled and extend a helping hand to the needy,..protecting the widow and the orphan and to make and preserve a record of the services of every member, and as far as possible of those of our comrades who have preceded us in eternity.
A Camp was formed in Elizabeth City, North Carolina, July 4, 1905, and was named W. F. Martin Camp

Note:
1. Camp 1590 Log Book, Museum of The Albemarle, Elizabeth City

#1590, United Confederate Veterans. It was named in memory of Colonel W. F. Martin, of Civil War fame. He lived in Elizabeth City. His old home is now part of the Twiford's Funeral Home,...on Church Street.

The rules for admittance to the local Camp were that a person had to be of good character and to have served honorably as a soldier or sailor of the Confederate States.

Initiation fee was fifty cents and the dues were fifteen cents quarterly. The annual per capita tax was ten cents. This was sent to the Grand Camp in New Orleans. An annual meeting was held the second Thursday in August. Regular meetings were held...the first Friday of January, April, July, and October.

Members joining this Camp were from Pasquotank and Camden Counties, with a few from Perquimans County. All of the veterans..of the Confederacy living in 1905 in this vicinity did not join the United Veterans organization, some probably from indifference,..and some being too feeble to get around.

A total of 52 became members of the W. F. Martin Camp #1590, UCV. Eight of these were from Perquimans, twenty-one were natives of Camden, and the balance were natives of Pasquotank. The Secretary of the Camp kept very good records. He wrote legibly, and he kept the roll up to date. He would record the date of death of the members, and when one would die, his family would be sent a certificate giving the name of the Camp, date of death, veteran's war records, and condolences from his comrades."

* * * * *

2

Committee on
drafting and formulating
Constitution,
and
By Laws.
of
Wm F. Martin Camp
No. 1590 U.C.V.

E. R. Outlaw, Chm
D. B. Bradford
John H. Burgess Sr.

30

Wm F Martin Camp #1590 U.C.V.

Camp Roll
Record for
1909
and
1910

Fees Dues, Etc. Etc.

D. B. Bradford   Commander

John H. Burgess   Adjutant

These page portions are from the original log book of the W. F. Martin Camp 1590, UCV, found in the Museum of the Albemarle, near Elizabeth City. The upper part has William H. Elliott's membership date. The lower part shows him deceased, a former Lt., Co. B, 68th N. C. T. Infantry.

A page from the log book of the W.F. Martin Camp, 1590.

On a hot August day, in 1910,
a number of aging Confederate
Veterans, shaded only by their
broad-brimmed soft black hats,
were observers of Camp 1590's
annual business meeting.

Induction into the Camp then
followed for some. My grandfather, William H. Elliott, was
among those in the group below
who joined the Camp that day.

He appears at left, and under
the arrow below.

A few Confederate Veterans were photographed beside the Pasquotank County Court House, on May 10, 1911. On that day the Confederate Monument was unveiled. Dr. D. H. Hill, L. L. D., President of A & M College, at Raleigh, gave the Memorial address. Following this was a veterans parade, and a bountiful lunch for all. In comparing the Camp photograph of August, 1910, with the above, I guess that my grandfather, William H. Elliott, may be kneeling at the extreme left in the front row. The beard, hat, and white shirt with no tie, are similar.

ELIZABETH CITY, NORTH CAROLINA, FRIDAY, MAY 12, 1911

Tribute to the Old Veterans on the day of the Erection of the Confederate Monument in E. City May 10, 1911

By Mrs. John Newbold, of Hertford.)

How it stirred our hearts to see them
The Veterans old and brave;
As they marched in meager number
And faced the young so gay,
Only a few of the old to muster
To the call of horn and drum,
But they bear a stamp of Courage
On their faces scarred and worn.
May the sons who take their places
Have hearts as brave and true,
And tread to martial music
Under the flag red, white, and blue .

Mrs. John Newbold, author of this poetic tribute, was formerly Enola Glenn Elliott, grandfather William's first child.

LIST OF OLD SOLDIERS

Confederate Veterans that formed a line of march at the unveiling of the Confederate Monument in Elizabeth City, May 10th 1911.

The following registered with the Tar Heel reporter.

The Soldiers	Their Captain	Their Colonel
Henry Brown	W. A. Duke	Wm. F. Martin
J. B. Cartwright	J. B. Fearing	"
Thos H. Tulford	Mc D. Lindsay	"
Abner W. Hale	Thos P. Sivals	P F. Farison
Willis W. Morrisette	Captain	J. W. Hinton
J. W. Brothers	A. P. White	Paul Farison
Geo. H. Wood	Wm. Nixon	John R. Cook
J. S. Henderson	L. E. Satterwaite	Sol. Williams
Geo. W. Eason	Jno. G. Wallice	V. D. Groner
Joseph N. Spense	D. A. Sawyer	H. M. Shaw
P. C. Creekmore	Saml D. Bell	D. D. Ferebee
W. L. Etheridge	Wm. A. Duke	W. F. Martin
James Evans	Thos. J. Jarvis	H. M. Shaw
J. L. Lawrence	J. B. Fearing	Wm. F. Martin
Joseph Carmine	On the IronClad Merrimack	
M. D. Gregory	F. M. Halstead	J. W. Hinton
Isaac Wood	Thomas Cahoon	Wm. F. Martin
N. G. Burgess	G. G. Luke	Paul F. Faison
James A. Mathews	A. P. White	" "
J. H. Sawyer	J. G. Hughes	E. C. Brabble
J. B. Leigh	D. Bell	D. D. Ferebee
Henry A. Tarkenton	Tom Cahoon	Wm. F. Martin
N. S. Burgess	G. G. Luke	Paul F. Faison
A. J. Baily	J. W. Hinton	H. M. Shaw
Joseph M. Haskett	J. B Fearing	Wm. F. Martin
J. H. Tuttle	Thomas H. Tamplin	J. W. Hinton
N. G. Davis	Caleb Walston	J. W. Hinton
James Anderson	B. C. Manley	Col. Cable
L. S. Sivals	Major Sanderlin	J W. Hinton
L. G. Pipkin	S. B. Barrington	Jno. D. Witford
W. N. Parker	John Booth	Col. Spruill
Zenas Fearing	J. B. Fearing	Wm. F Martin
R. F. Simpon	Tom Cahoon	Wm. F. Martin
J. Q. Etheridge	J. B Fearing	Wm. F. Martin
Jno. H. Burgess	J. B. Fearing	Wm. F. Martin
G. W. Hobbs	J. M: Whitson	H. M. Shaw
Wm. Cartwright	J. B. Fearing	Wm. F. Martin
Captain E. R. Outlaw	" "	
Edwin V. Ellis	Robt. Brinkley	Jno. R. Chamblis
D. B. Bradford	J. B. Fearing	Wm. F. Martin
A. H. Worth	" "	"
Joseph T. Spence	J. W. Hinton	H. M. Shaw
W. H. Elliott	F. M. Halstead	J. W. Hinton
Caleb Raper	Thos H. Tamplin	J. W. Hinton
William Kemp	Wm. Badam	J. W. More
Ab. A. Combs	Wm. Badam	J. W. More
W. D. Gregory	F. M. Halstead	J. W. Hinton
P. S. Shipp	Isaac Hall	Col. Wheelock Co. A
97th., New York Volunteers		

In January of 1914, grandfather William's health began to fail. His physician had seen him from time to time, since April of 1912, as infirmities of advanced age became evident.

Late in the day, on January 21, 1914, the doctor responded to a message from the family. Grandfather was seriously ill. In spite of all efforts to comfort and treat him, grandfather William died at midnight, on January 21, 1914, at age 73.

Most family members were present, with the exception of his two sons in New York state, William T. D., and Joseph K. Elliott. Although they received telegrams, transportation of the day prevented them from attending the funeral, on January 23rd. They arrived the next day. He was buried in the family plot on his farm, beside his last child, infant son, Roy. A headstone marks the grave.

ELLIOTT.—Bro. William H. Elliott at his home in Nixonton, N. C., on Janu 21, 1914, in his seventy-third year. leaves to mourn their loss a devoted wife seven children, had twelve grandchildre He was thrice married For many months prior to his death, he was a great sufferer.

He was a Confederate soldier, a member of Company A., Sixty-eighth N. C., of General Joseph E. Johnston's division, and served with credit to himself till the surrender. He was from time to time promoted till made first lieutenant.

For many years, he was an honored deacon and one of the most faithful members of the Woodville Baptist Church. He will be greatly missed by his family, friends, and his church. A good man, whose life was a blessing, has gone to his reward.

The funeral was conducted by his pastor from the residence, and the remains interred in the family burying ground, in the presence of a large concourse of sorrowing loved ones and friends.

May the Lord comfort and bless the bereaved family.—B. F. Bray, A. A. Butler, Hertford, N. C.

His obituary was published by the Elizabeth City newspaper. It noted his Confederate military service in the 68th Regiment, and said his final rank was that of Lieutenant.

WILLIAM H. ELLIOTT
Age 71, 1912

Shortly thereafter, the Camp prepared their customary Memoriam. It had become traditional to award these to the families of deceased former Confederate veterans. Inscribed was his rank of Lieutenant, Co. B, 68th Regiment, North Carolina Infantry, C. S. A. How strange that grandfather's family never received the Memoriam! It was discovered over sixty years later, as part of an exhibit at the Museum of the Albemarle near Elizabeth City.

A casual inquiry if there was a Confederate display produced a surprise. Right in the center of a large hexagonal glass case was an erect wooden pole. Hanging from a nail were several Memoriams. On top was my grandfather's. I learned that most of the exhibit was in custody of a Trust. Eventually the Museum became sole owners.

The Memoriam, thought lost, had never been presented to grandfather's family. As a consequence, I began a negotiation to procure this original link with grandfather's past. In a short time I was successful. After having been preserved by a graphic conservator, and safely framed, the Memoriam now hangs over my desk.

IN MEMORIAM
W. F. Martin Camp No. 1590 U. C. V.

Elizabeth City, N. C., _____ 1914

Whereas:--

In merciful kindness towards us all, it has pleased the Great Chieftain on High to remove from our camp fire on earth our beloved comrade _William H. Elliott_ _Lt._ _Co B. 68th Reg't N. Carolina Infantry C.S.A._ _"War for Southern Independence 1861–1865._

Therefore be it

Resolved 1st.:—That we, his comrades of the past, bow in humble submission to the inevitable will of "Him who doeth all things well" and say "Thy will be done."

Resolved 2nd.:—That our heart felt sympathies are extended to the bereaved family of our Comrade.

Resolved 3rd.:—That a copy of these resolution be published in the city papers~~~a coppy be sent to the family~~~and one be entered upon the records of this Camp.

Committee

Comrade E. R. Outlaw Chm   _Capt. D. B. Bradfort_

1st Lt. J. T. Spence,

One of dad's first duties, as man of the house, was to pay all
final expenses relating to grandfather's funeral. Foremost of the
few obligations, was the bill of Dr. F. H. Ziegler, Funeral Director
and Embalmer.

Telephone 182   STATEMENT   Established 1856

Elizabeth City, N. C., *Jan 24 1914*

Mr *J. K. Elliott*

To F. H. ZIEGLER, Dr.
Funeral Director and Embalmer
All Telegrams Promptly Attended to Day or Night
No. 204 South Road Street

Jan 22	Casket for W H Elliott,				$45.00
	Paid by				
	J. K. Elliott				
	Rec'd payment Jan 24th				
	F H Ziegler				

North Carolina State Board of Health
BUREAU OF VITAL STATISTICS

CERTIFICATE OF DEATH

6 10

PLACE OF DEATH

County _Pasquotank_

Township _Nixonton_

Town _____

Registration District No. _70-5922_

City _____ (No. _____ St.; _____ Ward)

File No. _____
Registered No. _4_

[If death occurred in a hospital or institution give its NAME instead of street and number.]

FULL NAME _William H. Eliott_

PERSONAL AND STATISTICAL PARTICULARS	MEDICAL CERTIFICATE OF DEATH

SEX _Male_   COLOR OR RACE _White_   SINGLE, MARRIED, WIDOWED, or DIVORCED (Write the word) _Married_

DATE OF DEATH _Jan_ (Month) _21_ (Day) _19__ (Year)

DATE OF BIRTH _Feb_ (Month) _10_ (Day) _1841_ (Year)

AGE _71_ yrs. _11_ mos. _11_ ds.   If LESS than 1 day, _____ hrs. or _____ min.

OCCUPATION
(a) Trade, profession, or particular kind of work _Farmer_
(b) General nature of industry, business, or establishment in which employed (or employer) _____

I HEREBY CERTIFY, That I attended deceased from _April_ 19 _15_ _Jan_ _21_ _19_

that I last saw _him_ alive on _Jan 21_ 19__

and that death occurred on the date above stated, at _12 P_ m.

The CAUSE OF DEATH* was as follows:

Arterio Sclerosis

(Duration) _Several_ mos.

EDUCATIONAL ATTAINMENTS _Common_

Contributory (Secondary) _Softening o Brain_

(Duration) _____ yrs. _____ mos.

BIRTHPLACE _Camden Co N.C_

(Signed) _A. Irving_
Jan 22 1917 (Address) _Eliz City N.C_

PARENTS

NAME OF FATHER _Dr Peter Eliott_

BIRTHPLACE OF FATHER (State or Country) _Camden Co N.C._

MAIDEN NAME OF MOTHER _Mary Brockett_

BIRTHPLACE OF MOTHER (State or Country) _Camden Co N.C_

*State the Disease Causing Death, or, in Deaths from Violent Causes
(1) Means of Injury; and (2) whether Accidental, Suicidal, or Homicidal

LENGTH OF RESIDENCE (For Hospitals, Institutions, Transients or Recent Residents)
At place of death _____ yrs. _____ mos. _____ ds.   In the State _____ yrs. _____ mos.
Where was disease contracted, if not at place of death? _____
Former or usual residence _____

THE ABOVE IS TRUE TO THE BEST OF MY KNOWLEDGE

(Informant) _Mrs Daniel Gregory_

(Address) _3911 Chamber Ave Norfolk Va_

Filed _Jan 26_ 19_17_ _L. L. Brockett_ Registrar

PLACE OF BURIAL OR REMOVAL _Nixonton Township_   DATE OF BURIAL _Jan 23_

UNDERTAKER _F H Ziegler_   ADDRESS _E City NC_

NORTH CAROLINA

PASQUOTANK COUNTY

    This is to certify that the foregoing (or annexed) instrument is

a true and correct copy of the original certificate on file in this Office.

    WITNESS my hand and Official Seal, this _7th_ day of

_____May_____, 1984.

J. C. Spence
Register of Deeds

By: _Dollie G. Summerour_
Deputy ~~Assistant~~

Grandfather William's personality and strength of character was inherited by each of his children.

Born to the frugality and simplicity of farm life, these basic values inherent to country living, were to become prominent factors in their adjustment to adulthood.

I came to know each of grandfather's children, excepting Enola Glenn, his eldest daughter. Members of the family told me in later years that Enola emulated her brothers and sisters in charm, love for the land, friendliness, sense of humor, expressions of hospitality, love for their families, and their strong fundamental religious beliefs.

In each home I visited, these traits were prominently evident. One was always expected to stay for at least one meal. A spare bedroom was always ready, and when it came time to depart, pleadings to stay another day were loud and long.

The magic of the land was to be influential in shaping the lives and careers of Enola, Tilla, Jack, Bill, Joe, Sarah, and Lucy.

Enola's married life was spent in the country. Jack worked in the forests, and sold land. Bill developed, and sold land, for homes. Joe also worked in the forests, and later developed, and sold land for homes, while living in the country. Sarah lived her entire life on a farm. Tilla spent her married life in the city. Lucy did the same.

Grandfather's widow, Dorothy, in her later years, made her home with her daughters, Sarah and Lucy, and with her son Joe. Most of the time, however, she lived with Sarah, much preferring the rural life. I can recall that in the late 1920's, dad would drive to Littleton, and bring grandmother back with him, to stay with us all through the winter months. Our country house was better suited for her comfort during those miserable winters.

Mrs Dorothy F Elliott

AT SARAH'S HOME   1935

Grandmother stayed with us each winter, until dad drove her back to Sarah's, for the last time, in the spring of 1935.

Dad and Sarah had made an application for a Confederate widow's pension, based upon grandfather William's Confederate service, and her deteriorated health. The physician who examined grandmother certified that she suffered from chronic Myocarditis, a weakening of the heart muscle.

In September, 1936, grandmother's application was approved, and increased, from CLASS B Pensioner, to CLASS A Pensioner. CLASS A required pensioners to be 'totally blind' or 'totally disabled, and confined to home.' As a young lady, grandmother's name was Dorothy Frances Keaton. After her first marriage, she was sometimes called Dorothy Keaton Price. She retained the name Keaton, upon marrying grandfather William, though at times she called herself Dorothy Frances Elliott.

My grandmother, Dorothy Keaton Elliott, died in Sarah's house, on October 16, 1937, at age 86.

Over the years, I have been drawn to the counties of Pasquotank and Camden. One who drives at random over the picturesque country roads, will frequently see markers commemorating historical events in this eastern section of North Carolina.

A wealth of Colonial lore awaits the visitor. Just a short buggy ride from grandfather's last farm on Body Road, would have brought him to a memorial site overlooking Halls Creek. A bronze tablet now marks where the Grand Assembly of Albemarle County met, on February 6, 1665.

Every time I have visited my relatives in Elizabeth City, I have arranged to enjoy the scenic rural roads of both counties. In doing so, I've also driven by grandfather's old farm on Body Road.

The farm house burned a short time after grandfather's death in 1914, but the property has been cultivated by someone nearby. Many of these visits have included moments of silent reflection beside the wrought-iron fence, which enclosed grandfather's grave.

While visiting Elizabeth City in the winter of 1983, I was in-

formed that damage to grandfather's grave was possible. Encroachment upon the old farm was likely, due to an increase of temporary housing nearby.

Before the day had ended, I asked Sam Twiford, of Twiford's Funeral Home, about the possibility of exhuming my grandfather's remains, and transferring them to a church cemetery near Littleton. His immediate response was, "Yes, we can disinter the remains at any time."

My cousin, William C. (Billy) Myrick in Littleton, said he would assume the responsibility for the interment in Calvary Church cemetery.

A Veterans Administration application for an upright white marble Confederate Veteran headstone, was endorsed by three of grandfather's grandchildren; William C. Myrick, Jr., his sister, Dorothy M. Pritchard, and myself.

Within a few weeks approval was received, The headstone arrived in Littleton about three months later. It would be Billy Myrick's job to place the stone.

During the first week of May, 1984, by prearrangement with Sam Twiford, the remains of grandfather Elliott were removed from the primitive, unattended plot, on his old farm. After preparation for transport, I chauffeured grandfather's remains from Elizabeth City to Littleton.

Billy Myrick had all in readiness. Grandfather's plot was in the midst of his family. Composing the small family group were; his wife, Dorothy; his daughter, Sarah; and his son, John Pool Elliott.

On a quiet, warm, and sunny country day, Billy and I performed a simple ceremony with dignity and reverence. Grandfather William was laid to final rest.

Behind the new headstone we placed the original stone face up, and flush with the grass. Billy then securely attached the bronze United Confederate Veterans marker to the headstone base. As a final gesture, we placed a small Confederate flag in the bronze marker. We had made payment of final honors to this Confederate Veteran.

As we walked back to our car, with tools in hand, I turned for a last glimpse. There, perched atop the new headstone, was a saucy Mockingbird, spreading his wings and singing his favorite melody. I imagine he was proud to have such a special perch upon which to serenade his private audience.

*   *   *   *   *

BIBLIOGRAPHY

OFFICIAL RECORDS OF THE UNION AND CONFEDERATE ARMIES
  OR, Serial I, Vols. IX; XVIII; XXIX, Pts. I, II; XXXIII; XXXVI,
Pt. III; XL, Pt. III; XLII, Pt. III; XLVI, Pt. II; XLVII, Pts. II,
III; LI, Pt. II.
  OR, Serial II, Vol. VI

REGIMENTAL HISTORIES
  North Carolina Regiments, 1861-1865, VOLS. I; II; III; IV; V; by
Walter Clark.

NORTH CAROLINA ROSTERS
  N. C. Troops, 1861-1865, Vol. VI, by Weymouth T. Jordan, Jr.
  N. C. Troops, Vols. II; IV; by John W. Moore.

CIVIL RECORDS
  Camden County Court House, N. C. Deed Books, T; BB; Z; AA; DD;
EE; FF.
  Pasquotank County Court House, N. C. Deed Books, V; 1817-1820;
17; 24; 32.

CENSUS
  1840 Camden Census, N. C.
  1850 Camden Census, N. C.
  1860 Pasquotank Census, N. C.

CHURCH RECORDS
  Parish of Christ Church, Elizabeth City, N. C.
  Woodville Baptist Church, Woodville, N. C.
  Episcopal Diocese of North Carolina, Parishioners letter, Decem-
ber issue, 1955.

PUBLICATIONS
  Marriages of Norfolk County, Virginia, 1706-1792, by Wingo.
  Three Hundred Years Along the Pasquotank, by Jesse Pugh.
  The American Beacon Daily, Norfolk, Virginia, April 6, 1821.
  The Raleigh Register, October 8, 1829.
  Camden County Marriage Register, N. C., 1848-1940
  Perquimans County Marriage Register, N. C., Vol. I, 1852-1940
  Pasquotank County Register of Deeds, Marriage Record, N. C.,
March 31, 1886.
  Tombstones & Epitaphs of Northeastern North Carolina, "Salem Bap-
tist Church Yard Burials," by Wilma C. Spence, Elizabeth City,
N. C.
  The Tar Heel Newspaper, Elizabeth City, N. C., Micro Film, May
1911, Pasquotank County Library, Elizabeth City.
  The Daily Advance Newspaper, Elizabeth City, N. C.

COLLECTIONS, PUBLIC & PRIVATE
  N. C. Archives, Records Room, C. W. Collections, Box 63
  Museum of the Albemarle, Elizabeth City, N. C.
  Weldon Memorial Library, Weldon, N. C.
  Pasquotank County Library, Elizabeth City, N. C.
  William W. Forehand, County Historian, Shiloh, N. C.
  Dorothy Myrick Pritchard, Elizabeth City, N. C.
  Eula Newbold Greenwood, Kittrell, N. C.
  Mrs. Herman Eley (Sarah Marie Morgan), Franklin, Va.
  Nancy Elliott (Mrs. John P. Elliott, Jr.), Richmond, Va.
  Robert Garrison Elliott, Daytona Beach, Fl.

    Descendants of Lt. William H. Elliott have honored his Confederate service with membership in the Sons of Confederate Veterans (SCV), United Daughters of the Confederacy (UDC), and the Military Order of the Stars and Bars (MOSB).

      Enola Glenn Newbold, REAL DAUGHTER, UDC
      Joseph Keaton Elliott, REAL SON, SCV, MOSB
      Lucy Elliott Morgan Bobbitt, REAL DAUGHTER, UDC
      Ruth Newbold Vail, GRANDDAUGHTER, UDC
      Myrtis Elliott Keppler, GRANDDAUGHTER, UDC
      Robert Garrison Elliott, GRANDSON, SCV, MOSB
      William Clements Myrick, Jr., GRANDSON, SCV, MOSB
      William Thomas Duke Elliott, Jr., GRANDSON, SCV, MOSB
      Kent M. Pritchard, GREAT GRANDSON, SCV, MOSB
      Robert G. Barnes, GREAT GRANDSON, SCV
      R. Steven Elliott, GREAT GRANDSON, SCV
      Arthur B. Savage, GREAT GRANDSON, SCV
      R. James Kolmer, Jr., GREAT GREAT GRANDSON, SCV, MOSB

INDEX

African Brigade, Union, 34
Albemarle, C. S. S. Ram, Conf., 16, 73
Anderson, Lt. Col. Archer, Conf., 61, 62, 68, 69
Armistead, Col. Frank S., Conf., 64
Ashby Harbor, Roanoke Island, N. C., 9, 10
Askew, Capt. Levi, Conf., 38
Averasboro, Harnett Co., N. C., 65
Avery, Capt. William B., Union, 15

Babcock, John C., Union, 42
Bagley, Maj. William H., Conf., 43
Baker, Gen. Lawrence S., Conf., 21, 37, 63
Bakersville, Mitchell Co., N. C., 70, 71
Banks, James, 96
Barco, Alex G., Conf., 72
Barden, Richard, 96
Barnes, Brig. Gen. James, Union, 26, 27, 30, 34
Barnes, Robert G., 126
Bartlett, William, 5
Beauregard, Gen. P. G. T., Conf., 43
Bentonville, Johnston Co., N. C., 63, 65, 67
Bertie County, N. C., 38
Bird, Lt. W. E. A., Union, 25, 26
Bobbitt, Eugene C., 92
Bobbitt, Lucy Elliott Morgan, 105. 126
Body Road, Pasquotank Co., N. C., 93, 94, 96,
   101, 122
Bond, Capt. R. H. L., Conf., 38
Bragg, Gen. Braxton, Conf., 41, 48, 50, 62, 63,
   65, 66, 69
Bray, B. F., Conf., 72
Bright, Daniel, Conf., 19, 20
Brockett's. 1
Brockett, Jonathon A., 3, 80, 83
Brockett, Lydia, 80
Brockett, Mary, 2
Brooks, George W., 24, 33
Brown, Thomas J., Conf., 64
Buffalo, N. Y., 79, 80
Buffaloes, 60, 61
Burgess, Cornelius, 17
Burgess, John, 80
Burgess, John Jr., 80, 81
Burgess, Nicholas, 17
Burgess, Peter, 17
Burgess, Stephen, 17
Burgess, Tamar, 1
Burgess, V. E., 81
Burnside, Gen. Ambrose, Union, 7, 9, 12, 14
Bushnell, Frank F., 35, 36
Butler, Gen. Benjamin, Union, 32, 33, 34, 39,
   49, 74
Butler's Bridge, Martin Co., N. C., 50, 51, 52,
   53, 54, 55, 60, 61, 67, 70, 71

Caho, 4th. Sgt. W. T., Conf., 63
Camden County, N. C., 1, 2, 14, 15, 17, 18, 19,
   21, 27, 34, 35, 36, 38, 44, 71, 73, 74, 76,
   77, 79, 80, 119, 122, 125
Camp Baker, Martin Co., N. C., Conf., 53
Cartwright, John, 17
Chaffin's Farm, Va., Conf., 49
Chappell, Capt., Conf., 41
Cherry, Capt., Conf., 41
Chowan County, N. C., 24, 32, 34, 38
Chowan River, N. C., 19, 32
Clark, William H., 33
Cobb's Mill, Jones Co., N. C., 67
Coniho Creek, Martin Co., N. C., 52, 54
Cox, Gen. J. D., Union, 64, 66
Cox's Bridge, Johnston Co., N. C., 63, 71
Currituck County, N. C., 14, 27, 32, 34

Daily Advance Newspaper, Elizabeth City, N. C.
   36, 72, 125
Dare County, N. C., 38
Dauge, Gen. Peter, Revolutionary War, 1
Daughtry, Capt. W. M., Conf., 38
Davis, George, 99
Davis, Maj. R. S., Union, 40
Davis, Thomas, 96
Daytona Beach, Florida, 88
Draper, Col. Alonzo G., Union, 30
Duke, James Edward, 74, 83, 84
Duke, Martha Jane, 74, 75, 76, 79, 80
Duncan, Ithrum, 17
Duncan, Wilson, 17

Edenton, Chowan Co., N. C., 21, 75
Ehringhaus, John C., 33
Eley, Herman, 92
Eley, Mrs. Herman (Marie Morgan), 92, 126
Elizabeth City, Pasquotank Co., N. C., 1, 5,
   12, 13, 14, 15, 16, 17, 18, 19, 21, 24, 25,
   32, 33, 36, 70, 71, 72, 73, 88, 92, 96, 107,
   116, 122, 124
Elliott, Charles E., 76
Elliott, Capt. Charles Grice, Conf., 6, 12, 13,
   73
Elliott, Charles T. (Tillett), 2
Elliott, Dorothy Keaton, 84, 85, 87, 91, 92,
   101, 104, 120, 121, 124
Elliott, Edna Garrison, 81, 88, 103, 104,
   105, 106
Elliott, Enola Catherine, 78
Elliott, Enola Glenn, 74, 75, 84, 86, 87, 120,
   126
Elliott, Gilbert, I, 1, 6
Elliott, Lt. Gilbert, II, Conf., 6, 12, 13,
   16, 73
Elliott, Harriett, 80, 102, 103
Elliott, James Duke, 78, 103
Elliott, John (Jack) Pool, Sr., 77, 78, 86,
   87, 93, 94, 97, 99, 100, 103, 120, 124
Elliott, John Pool, Jr., 2, 78, 103, 126
Elliott, Capt. John T., Conf., 16, 18, 20,
   24, 39
Elliott, Joseph Keaton, 2, 80, 87, 88, 91, 93,
   94, 97, 99, 100, 104, 106, 115, 118, 120, 126
Elliott, Rev. Josiah, 85
Elliott, Lucy Marie, 92, 101, 120, 126
Elliott, Marion (Polly) Hill, 78, 103
Elliott, Mary Brockett, 2, 3, 4, 5, 6, 74, 77,
   80, 82, 84, 119
Elliott, Mary Jane (Mollie), 2, 4, 5, 6, 76,
   77, 78, 81, 82, 83, 84
Elliott, Mary Matilda (Tilla), 77, 86, 91
Elliott, Myrtis, 78, 103
Elliott, Myrtis Myrick, 103
Elliott, Nancy (Mrs. John P. Elliott, Jr.),
   2, 126
Elliott, Peter, I, 1
Elliott, Peter, II, 1, 2, 3, 4, 5, 6
Elliott, Robert Garrison, 29, 104, 105, 126
Elliott, R. Steven, 126
Elliott, Roy F., 97, 115
Elliott, Sarah Berry, 91, 92, 101, 104, 120
Elliott, Sarah Grice, 6
Elliott, Tamar Burgess, 1
Elliott, Warren Grice, 6
Elliott, William, son of Gilbert Elliott, I, 6
Elliott, William, son of Peter Elliott, I, 1
Elliott, Lt. William Harrison, Conf., frontis-
   piece, 2, 5, 6; 1st enlistment, 12; captured-
   paroled, 13; 14, 20; 2nd enlistment, 21, 22,

23; 29; promotion from 3rd Sgt. to 1st Sgt.,
40; clothing issue, 44, 45, 46; 68; promotion to Lt., discharged, 70; 71, 72, 73; 1st
marriage, 74, 75, 76, 77, 78, 79, 80; 2nd
marriage, 81; 82, 83, 84; 3rd marriage, 85;
86, 87, 88, 89, 90, 91, 92, 93, 94, 95, 96,
97, 98, 99, 100, 101, 106, 107; joins U. C. V.
Camp 1590, 111, 112; 113, 114; death, 115;
116, 117, 118, 119, 120, 121, 122, 123, 124,
126
Elliott, William Thomas Duke, Sr., 79, 80, 86,
87, 93, 94, 103, 115, 120
Elliott, William T. Duke, Jr., 80, 102, 103,
126
Etheridge, Willis, 5
Evans, 4th Corp. John W., Conf., 38, 41, 43,
51, 67

Fearing, Isaiah, 33
Forehand, William W., 2, 29, 35, 36, 107, 126
Fort Bartow, Roanoke Island, N. C., Conf., 9, 10
Fort Branch map, Conf., 56, 71
Fort Branch (Rainbow Banks), Martin Co., N. C.,
Conf., 50, 51, 52, 53, 55, 57, 58, 63, 64,
68, 70, 71
Fort Fisher, Brunswick Co., N. C., Conf., 63
Fort Huger, Roanoke Island, N. C., Conf., 13
Fort Ocracoke, Hyde Co., N. C., Conf., 12
Fort Wadsworth, N. Y., Union, 73
Fortress Monroe, Virginia, Union, 26, 39
Foster, Gen. J. G., Union, 11, 24, 25
Franklin, Va., 92

Gates County, N. C., 32, 34, 38
Gatlin, Brig. Gen. Richard C., Conf., 37, 70
Gee, Maj. John H., Conf., 46, 48
Georgia Regiment, 62nd, Conf., 19
Gilmer, Col. John A., Conf., 46
Goldsboro, Wayne Co., N. C., 21, 63, 64, 65, 66,
67, 68, 70, 71
Granberry, Simon, 96
Grand Assembly of Albemarle County, N. C., 122
Grandy, Capt. Cyrus W., Conf., 38
Grandy, N. G., 76
Grant, Gen. U. S., Union, 49
Gray, Mary (Polly), 74
Greenville, Pitt Co., N. C., 67
Greenwood, Eula Newbold Nixon, 2, 5, 75, 126
Gregory, Major, 11, 20, 25
Gregory, Major D., Conf., 22, 23, 72
Gregory, Silas F., Conf., 11, 25, 26
Gregory, Tim, Conf., 15
Gregory, Willoughby D., Conf., 72
Guerrilla Island, Camden Co., N. C., 28, 29

Halifax, Halifax Co., N. C., 87
Halley's Landing, N. C., 16
Halls Creek, Pasquotank Co., N. C., 94, 95,
98, 122
Halls Creek Methodist Church, 94
Halstead, Lt. F. M., Conf., 21, 38, 114
Hamilton, Martin Co., N. C., 50, 51, 52, 53,
60, 61, 70, 71
Harrell, Joseph, 99
Hatteras Inlet, Hyde-Dare Co., N. C., 7, 12
Heath, Jack, Conf., 24
Hebert, Gen. Louis H., Conf., 50
Henningsen, Col. E. C., Conf., 14
Hertford, Perquimans Co., N. C., 14, 38, 75,
80, 81
Hertford Academy, Perquimans Co., N. C., 95
Hill, Dr. D. H., 113

Hill, Gen. D. H., Conf., 64
Hill, Maj. Gabriel H., Conf., 12, 13
Hinton, Col. James W., Conf., 20, 21, 24, 37,
39, 41, 43, 48, 51, 53, 60, 61
Hinton, Capt. Joseph, Conf., 51, 53, 61
Hoke, Gen. Robert F., Conf., 62, 64, 65, 66,
67, 68, 69
Holmes, Gen. T. H., Conf., 49
Hopewell, Va., 92
Horton, Rev. O. C., 81
Howard, Col. W. A., Union, 15
Humphreys, Maj. Gen. A. A., Union, 42

Indiantown, Camden Co., N. C., 25, 27, 29,
30, 31

Jackson, George W., 96
Jackson, Northampton Co., N. C., 37, 40, 71
Jennings, W. H., 100
Johnson, Gen. Bushrod, Conf., 43
Johnston, Capt. George H., Union, 21, 30
Johnston, Gen. Joseph E., Conf., 67, 69
Jones' Mill, Camden Co., N. C., 16
Jordan, Pvt. Samuel, Union, 20, 39
Jorden, T. H., 78

Keaton, Dorothy Frances, 121
Keaton, Joseph Zachariah, 85, 87, 97
Kent, Capt. William L., Union, 24, 25
Keogh, Capt. Richard, Conf., 38
Keppler, Myrtis Elliott, 126
Kight, Paul, 36
Kinston, Lenoir Co., N. C., 49, 63, 64, 65, 66,
67, 70, 71
Kolmer, R. James, Jr., 126

Lamb, Lt. Wilson G., Conf., 65
Lawrence, Capt. Lewis O., Conf., 44
Leary, Alex, 29, 36
Lee, Gen. Robert E., Conf., 48, 49, 50, 69
Leventhrope, Gen. Collett, Conf., 37
Lewis, Col. William, Union, 25, 26
Lister, Israel, 99
Lister, Will, 99
Little River, N. C., 16, 17, 91
Littleton, Halifax Co., N. C., 78, 87, 91,
104, 120, 123, 124

Mallory, Stephen R., Conf., 16
Mangum, Rev. A. W. (Chaplain), Conf., 48
Manteo, Dare Co., N. C., 38
Martin, Gen. James G., Conf., 48
Mebane, Capt. John T., Conf., 38
Memoriam, Lt. William Harrison Elliott, Conf.,
117
Mix, Col. S. H., Union, 24
Moore, Capt. M. V., Conf., 51
Moore's Roster, Conf., N. C., 38
Morgan, Charles Elliott, 92, 105
Morgan, Joseph, 17
Morgan, Lucy Elliott, 92, 105, 126
Morgan, Nix, 92, 97, 105
Morgan, Sarah Marie, 92, 105
Morganton, Burke Co., N. C., 43, 46, 70, 71
Morris, John S., 99, 100
Morrisette, C. B., Conf., 72
Morrisette, Sgt. T. L., Conf., 21
Morrisette, William G., 76
Morrisette, Lt. Willis W., Conf., 21
Moss, Thomas, 17
Munden, Mrs. Phoebe, 20, 39
Munden, Lt. W. J., Conf., 20

Murfreesboro, Hertford Co., N. C., 37, 39, 70, 71

Museum of the Albemarle, Pasquotank Co., N. C., 72, 111, 116, 126

Muster Roll, Capt. Sanderlin's Company, Conf., 22, 23

McPherson, Dr. Elizabeth, 3

Myrick, Dorothy Kathryn, 91, 104

Myrick, Myrtis, 77, 78, 99

Myrick, Sarah Elliott, 91, 104, 120, 121, 124

Myrick, William C., Sr., 91

Myrick, William C., Jr., 91, 104, 123, 124, 126

Nethercutt, Col. John H., Conf., 66

New Bern, Craven Co., N. C., 18, 24, 63, 64, 66, 69, 70

Newby's Bridge, Perquimans Co., N. C., 14

Newbold, Enola Elliott, 95, 102

Newbold, Henry Clay, 74

Newbold, James, 81

Newbold, John, 74, 75, 87, 102

Newbold, John Henry, 75

Newbold, K. R., 81

Newbold, Margaret, 75

Newbold, Martha Eula, 75

Newbold, Mary E., 81

Newbold, Mary Elliott, 75, 81

Newbold, Ruth Vernon, 75

Newbold, W. N., 81

Newbold, Virginia (Jennie) E., 80, 81, 82

Newport, Carteret Co., N. C., 40

Nixonton, Pasquotank Co., N. C., 16, 17, 24, 25, 32, 84, 85, 87, 91, 92, 96, 98

Norfolk, Va., 7, 20, 26, 27, 30, 31, 34, 39, 73, 77, 79, 87, 99

North Carolina Archives, 126

North Carolina Battalions, Conf., 1st Jr. Reserves, 64, 69; 1st N. C. Bn, 69; 1st Heavy Arty Bn, 37; 1st Bn Reserves, 41; Mallett's Bn, 41; 14th Cav Bn, 37; 15th Cav Bn (Wynn's), 37; 6th N. C. Cav, 64

North Carolina Batteries, Conf., Dicken's Btry, 64; Lee's (Alabama) Btry, 50, 51, 52, 64; 10th N. C. Arty, 64

North Carolina Brigades, Conf., Colquitt's, Hagood, 66; Martin-Kirkland, 13, 73; Kirkland's Brig (42nd Reg), 66

North Carolina Militia, Conf., 1st Brigade, 14; 15

North Carolina Regiments, Conf., 1st, 40; 4th, 40; 6th, 48; 7th N. C. Vols, 12; 8th, 37, 40; 10th, 51, 62, 64; 17th First Org., 12, 13, 71; 17th Second Org., 13, 16, 65, 73; 19th, 40; 21st, 40; 25th, 40, 43; 42nd, 64; 44th, 40; 49th, 40; 50th, 50; 51st, 40; 54th, 40; 59th, 40; 61st, 40; 65th, 50, 51, 52; 66th, 20, 21, 39, 66; 67th, 37, 49, 50, 64, 66, 67, 68, 69; 68th, 21, 37, 39, 40, 41, 43, 44, 46, 48, 49, 50, 51, 52, 54, 60, 61, 62, 63, 64, 66, 67, 68, 69, 70, 71, 72, 111, 116; 70th, 51, 52, 53; 79th, 37

North Carolina State Guards (Home Guards), 7, 21, 35, 37

Old Trap, Camden Co., N. C., 16

Ord, Gen. Edward O. C., Union, 49

Oregon Inlet, Dare Co., N. C., 8, 12, 71

Overman, Alma, 99

Overman, Mary, 96

Overman, R. F., 33

Overton, Elijah, 100

Overton, Mary, 99

Palmer, Gen. Innis Newton, Union, 40, 66

Parkville, Perquimans Co., N. C., 24, 81

Pasquotank County, N. C., 1, 5, 13, 14, 16, 17, 21, 32, 33, 37, 38, 81, 84, 89, 96, 99, 100, 113, 122

Pasquotank County Library, Elizabeth City, N. C., 126

Peck, Maj. Gen. John J., Union, 24

Perkins, John C., Conf., 72

Perquimans County, N. C., 12, 14, 21, 24, 32, 34, 74, 80, 81, 83, 84, 87, 89, 96

Pickett, Maj. Gen. George E., Conf., 19

Plymouth, Washington Co., N. C., 16, 50, 51, 52

Point Lookout, Md., 21

Pool, Col. Stephen D., Conf., 63

Pool, Dr. William G., 33

Poole, Capt. Simon B., Conf., 38

Porter, Capt. F. E., Union, 18

Powell's Point, Currituck Co., N. C., 27, 30

Price, Dorothy Keaton, 25, 85, 93, 121

Price, John T., 25, 85

Price, William A., 24

Pritchard, Dorothy Myrick, 123, 126

Pritchard, Kent M., 126

Pugh, Jesse Forbes, 35

Pugh, Randy, 36

Raleigh, N. C., 19, 43, 49, 113

Ransom, Gen. Matt W., Conf., 37, 43

Richmond, Va., 26, 41, 49, 78, 103

Roanoke Island, Dare Co., N. C., 7, 9, 10, 13, 14, 15, 17, 30, 31, 33, 71

Roberts, Capt. E. Dewees, Union, 18, 19, 21

Rochester, N. Y., 79, 80, 88

St. Petersburg, Fl., 88

Salem Baptist Church, Pasquotank Co., N. C., 81

Salisbury, N. C., 46, 47, 48, 50, 70, 71

Sanderlin, Lillie, 83

Sanderlin, Capt. Willis B., Conf., 14, 19, 20, 21, 22, 26, 29, 30, 31, 35, 40; promoted to Major, 43; 46, 71

Sanders, Capt. E. C., Union., 15, 16, 17

Sandy Hook, Camden Co., N. C., 30

Savage, Arthur B., 126

Sawyer, Daniel, 77, 102

Sawyer, Dorothy E., 77

Sawyer, Tilla Elliott, 102, 119, 120

Sawyer, Richard Leigh, 77

Schofield, Gen. John McAllister, Union, 63, 66

Shaw, Col. Henry M., Conf., 10, 11, 13

Shaw, Capt., Conf., 41

Shawboro, Camden Co., N. C., 11

Sherman, Gen. William T., Union, 63, 64, 65, 66

Sherrod House, Martin Co., N. C., 50, 53, 61

Shiloh map, Camden Co., N. C., 4, 28

Shiloh, Camden Co., N. C., 1, 2, 3, 4, 5, 6, 15, 16, 18, 20, 21, 27, 28, 30, 46, 73, 74, 77, 78, 80, 83, 107

Smithfield, Johnston Co., N. C., 63, 65, 67, 70, 71

Snyder, Arletta, 79, 103

South Mills, Camden Co., N. C., 19, 26, 27, 37

South West Creek, Jones Co., N. C., 64, 66, 67, 70, 71

Spence, J. C., 100

Spring Green Church, Martin Co., N. C., 50, 51, 55, 61

Stanton, Edwin M., 33

State Partisan Rangers, N. C., 26, 35

Stevens, Lt. Enoch, Conf., 21

Strange, Robert, Conf., 41
Stratton, Maj. Franklin A., Union, 19
Sumner, C. F., 81
Sutton, Capt. William M., Conf., 38
Symond Creek, Pasquotank Co., N. C., 86, 87, 88

Tamplin, Capt. Thomas H., Conf., 38
Tar Heel Newspaper, Elizabeth City, N. C., 114, 125
Tarboro, Edgecombe Co., N. C., 51, 52, 60, 61, 63, 67, 70, 71
Tayloe, Capt. Langley, Conf., 38
Taylor, Capt. Hillary, Conf., 38
Tillett, Samuel B., 5, 6
Twiford, Sam, 123

Union Naval Ships, Ceres, Eagle, Putnam, Virginia, 14; Lancer, 15; Patty Martin, Southfield, 16; Patty Martin, Whitehead, 17; Arrow, Emily, 18; Flora Temple, 31
Union Regiments, 8th Mass., 18; 23rd Mass. Inf Vols, 24; 27th Mass., 64; 55th Mass., 34; 5th Penn. Cav, 25; 11th Penn. Vol Cav, 18, 19, 21; 15th Ct., 64; 5th Oh., 20; 3rd N. Y. Cav, 24; 9th N. Y., 14; 6th N. H., 14; 1st N. C. Inf, 15; 1st, 2nd, 3rd, N. C., colored, 34; 1st, 5th, 10th, U. S., colored, 34
Upton, Samuel, 5, 74

Vail, Joseph Matthew, 75
Vail, Ruth Newbold, 75, 126
Vance, Gov. Zebulon B., N. C., 19, 31, 34, 49 50

Wallis, Maj. J. W., Union, 17, 18
Walston, Capt. Caleb B., Conf., 38
Walston, Mollie, 2, 5, 76, 77, 78, 81, 82, 83, 84
Walston, Joseph S., 5, 76, 78, 79, 84
Walston, William P., Conf., 72
Walter Clark's N. C. Regimental Histories, 38
Washington, D. C., 77
Washington, N. C., 50
Weeks, Mrs. Elizabeth, 20, 39
Weeks, Pvt. Pender, Conf., 20
Weldon map, N. C., 42
Weldon, Halifax Co., N. C., 21, 37, 40, 41, 43, 63, 70, 71
Weldon Memorial Library, Weldon, N. C., 126
Wessells, Brig. Gen. H. W., Union, 18
Wharton, Lt. Col. Rufus W., Conf., 66
Whitehead, Mary, 74
Whitehurst, James, 36
Whitford, Col. John N., Conf., 66, 68, 69
Whiting, Maj. Gen. W. H. C., Conf., 50, 61, 62
Wild, Brig. Gen. Edward A., Union, 19, 21, 26, 27, 29, 30, 31, 33, 34, 35, 39, 74
William F. Martin Camp 1590, UCV, Elizabeth City, N. C., 70, 72, 107, 108, 109, 110, 111, 112, 117
Williams, A. H., Conf., 72
Williams, Grandy & Co., 78
Williamston, Martin Co., N. C., 50, 60, 61, 63, 71
Wilmington, New Hanover Co., N. C., 50, 61, 63, 64, 66
Wilson, Wilson Co., N. C., 67, 70, 71
Wilson, W. J., 36
Winslow, Henry, 57
Wise, Gen. Henry A., Conf., 14

Wise's (Wyse) Fork, Jones Co., N. C., 63, 64, 66, 67, 68
Woodville Baptist Church, Perquimans Co., N. C., 94
Woodville, Perquimans Co., N. C., 24, 32, 94
Wright, Dempsey, 17
Wright, William, 16
Wyse Fork map, Jones Co., N. C., 65

Yellowley, Lt. Col. Edward C., Conf., 37, 40, 44, 60, 61, 63, 66

Ziegler, Dr. F. H., 118, 119

NAMES. PRESENT AND ABSENT. (Privates in alphabetical order.)	RANK.	ENLISTED.			LAST PAID.			NAMES. PRESENT.
		WHEN.	WHERE.	BY WHOM.	PERIOD.	BY WHOM.	TO WHAT TIME.	

NAMES	RANK	WHEN	WHERE	BY WHOM	PERIOD	BY WHOM	TO WHAT TIME	NAMES PRESENT
Sawyer Nathan	Private	July 7	Camden	Capt Sanderlin	3 yr	Capt Sawrie	to 30 Apl	Furlough in
Staples Caleb	"	Dec. 1 63	"	"	"	due from Enlist		Absent Sick in
Salyer Samuel	"	July 9 63	"	"	"	Capt Sawrie	30 Apl Salyer Samu	On Guard
Sawyer Coston S	"	Dec. 1	"	"	"	"	" " Sawyer Coston S	On Guard
Sanderlin Enoch	"	Mch 10 64	Murfees	"	"	"	" " Sanderlin Enoch	On Guard
Taylor Chas	"	July 7	Camden Co	"	"	due from Enlist		Prisoner
Throop George	"	July "	"	"	"	"		"
Tillett Jonathan	"	Dec. 1 63	"	"	"			Detach Service
Tillett J. B.	"	July 7 63	"	"	"	Capt Sawrie	30 Apl	Prisoner War
Whitehurst Saml	"	" "	"	"	"	due from Enlist		Prisoner War
Wilson Isaac	"	" "	"	"	"			"
Wilson, Mr. R.	"	Apr 25 64	Garysburg	S	"	" " Wilson Mr R.	On Guard
Williams Isel	"	Jan 15	Murfreesboro	"	"	Capt Sawrie	30 Apl Williams Isel C.	Sick in L
Woodhouse Major	"	Oct 8	Camden Co	"	"	"	30 Apl Woodhouse Major	On Guard
Wyatt John C	Musn	Nelson	"			due from Enlist	Wyatt Jno	On Guard

Discharged
Collins Edward
Jones Isaac

Dropped under order of Se[n]
"

Transferred
Grandy Abner Dønald
Hughes Marshall

Transferred to Co "G"
3 Dec 1864

Died
Banks Tilly
Whitehurst Henry

Deserted
Brown Casy
Brown George
Smith Virginius

Of the 68
From the [...]
To the 30
R[ece]d (A. &)

Joined the 1[...]

RECORD OF EVENTS WHICH MAY BE NECESSARY OR USEFUL FOR FUTURE REFERENCE AT THE WAR DEPARTMENT, OR FOR PRESENT INFORMATION.

Sa

I certify, on honor, that this M[uster Roll]
that it exhibits the true state of [...]
("B") of the 68th [...]
period herein mentioned; that the [...]
rate and just; and that the "Rec[apitulation]"
required by Regulations and the R[...]
STATION: Weldon,
DATE:

I certify, on honor, that I ha[ve]
minutely inspected the company, th[...]
unto annexed:

DISCIPLINE: Ba[d]
INSTRUCTION: Goo[d]
MILITARY APPEARANCE: In[...]
ARMS: Ex[...]
ACCOUTREMENTS: Co[...]
CLOTHING: Goo[d]